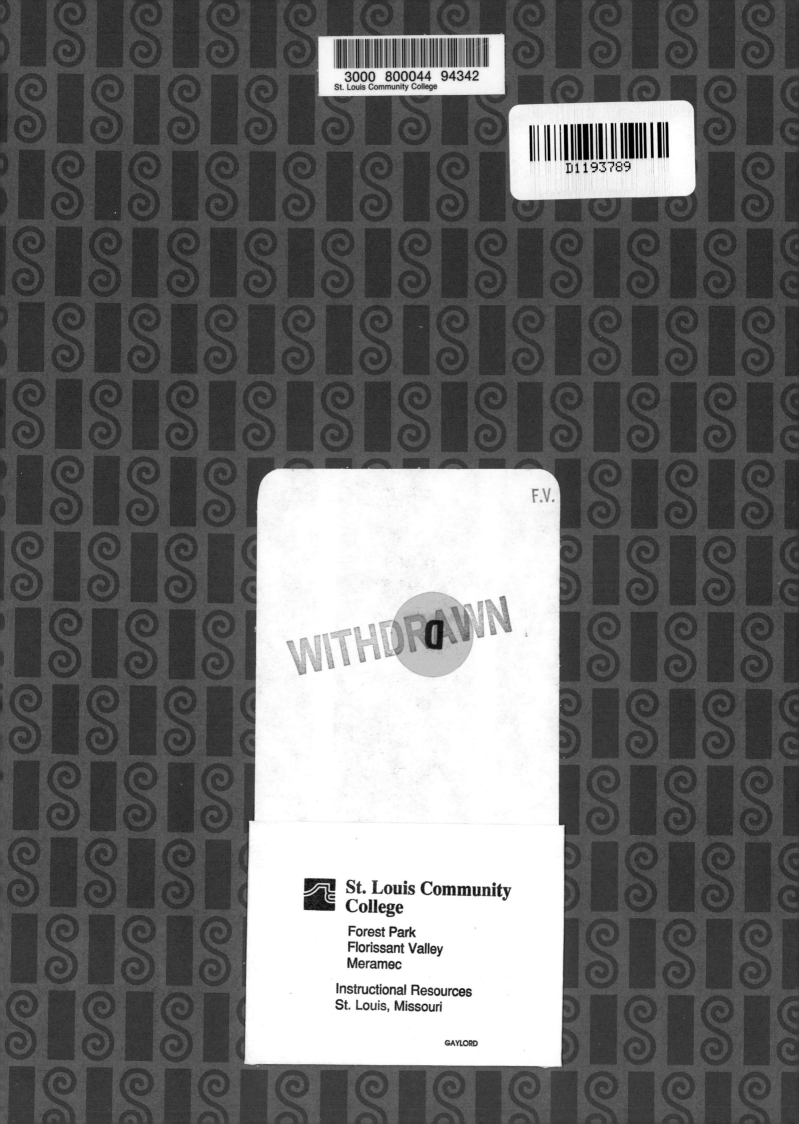

THE SOCIETY OF ILLUSTRATORS
39TH ANNUAL OF AMERICAN ILLUSTRATION

ILLUSTRATORS 39

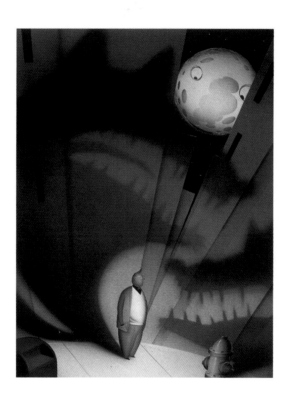

From the exhibition held in the galleries of the
Society of Illustrators Museum of American Illustration
128 East 63rd Street, New York City
February 8 — April 12, 1997

Society of Illustrators, Inc.
128 East 63rd Street, New York, NY 10021

ISBN 0-8230-6461-1
Library of Congress Catalog Card Number 59-10849

Distributed to the trade in the United States by:
Watson-Guptill Publications
1515 Broadway
New York, NY 10036

Published and distributed throughout the rest of the world by:
Rotovision Sales Office
Sheridan House
112/116A Western Road
Hove BN3 1DD ENGLAND
Tel. + 44 1273 727268
Fax + 44 1273 727269

Illustrators 39 is published for the Society of Illustrators by:
Rotovision, SA
7 rue du Bugnon
1299 Crans
Switzerland

Cover design by Wendell Minor
Cover painting by Bill Mayer
Interior Design by Harish Patel

Printed in Singapore

Photo Credits: Chesley Bonestell by John Gorman, David Bowers by Mike Robinson,
Vincent DiFate by Murray Tinkelman, Leo & Diane Dillon by Lee Dillon,
William Joyce by Neil Johnson, Gary Kelley by Bill Witt,
Barbara Nessim by Heather McGuire, Robert Neubecker by Kit Latham,
Fred Otnes by Marianne Barcellona, Joe Sorren by Stephen Schweitzer,
Chris Spollen by Marianne Barcellona

THE SOCIETY OF
ILLUSTRATORS
39TH ANNUAL OF
AMERICAN
ILLUSTRATION

ILLUSTRATORS
39

Published by Rotovision S.A.

PRESIDENT'S MESSAGE

Portrait by John Rush

John Bergstrom of American Showcase with Wendell Minor, Chairman of the 39th Annual (right) and Murray Tinkelman, Assistant Chair (left). American Showcase was once again the Exclusive Sponsor of Awards Galas for the Annual Exhibition.

american **showcase**

Illustrators 39 is likely to be the best exhibition of illustrative art you'll see this year. Once more, another show and another opportunity for illustration's finest to strut its stuff. To be sure, we're not perfect, but the Society, through the efforts of its Past Chairmen's Committee, strives mightily to improve these exhibitions with each passing year, carefully attempting to strike a balance between what the juries collectively feel is the best of what's submitted with what is most representative of illustration's constantly changing aesthetic landscape. Clearly, we all can't be happy with the results, for that is the inherent nature of the beast. If we all thought alike, all responded to the same artistic standards, we'd all paint the same way and illustration in America would become as lackluster and pointless as contemporary television. Once, when I was depressed about the first negative letter of comment I'd ever received, an editor friend of mine told me that if the readers didn't write in from time to time to complain, then we weren't doing our job—we weren't entertaining them, we were merely boring them. Those who are startled or upset by something new often come to embrace that new idea in time. A good case in point is Surrealism—or Conceptualism, if you will—once the rage in mainstream fine art but regarded as too outré for commercial picture making, it fairly dominated illustration in the '70s and '80s and is still very much alive as we head toward the new millennium.

We extend our thanks to Chairman Wendell Minor, his Assistant Chair, Murray Tinkelman, and to the many top talents who gave selflessly of their time and good judgement as jurors to make Illustrators 39 the grand display it is. Our thanks, too, to the Society's incredible staff who tirelessly deal with the mountain of submissions, and traffic manage the arriving and departing artwork year after year without complaint and with preternatural efficiency. The Publications Committee, under the guiding hand of Chairman Jerry McConnell, is to be commended too, for producing the unequivocal showcase book of our industry.

Congratulations to all of you with work in the show, for in every respect you have made this whole event possible through your faith in the selection process and by virtue of the sheer excellence of your art. As our Annual Exhibitions continue to grow and submissions soar, it becomes increasingly more difficult to be chosen from among the veritable ocean of work that arrives each year at our doorstep. You've done much to be proud of and you have given the rest of us yet another lofty standard to strive toward.

Vincent DiFate
President
1995 - 1997

CHAIRMAN'S MESSAGE

Portrait by John Rush

I believe I am the only past President of the Society of Illustrators to chair the annual exhibition after his presidency and not before, which leads me to think of a few more "firsts" for the 39th Annual of American Illustration. Anita Kunz was the first woman to create an illustration for the call for entries poster. Michael Whalen was the first artist to win a gold medal for a digital illustration. The 39th Annual was the first to be announced on the internet. Bill Mayer's art was chosen for the cover of this year's annual book. I had the privilege of designing the cover. It was the first time two Ringling School of Art and Design graduates have ever collaborated on an annual cover, and most likely will be the last. Or does lightning strike in the same place twice?

David McCullough once told me that it takes at least 50 years for one to gain a clear perspective on any event in history. As the Society of Illustrators fast approaches its one hundredth anniversary in 2001, I believe my perspective is very clear on the importance of the Society as custodian and documentor of the field of American illustration. Our annual exhibition continues to be the hallmark of the industry, and serves as a very valuable time capsule for today's artists and future generations of artists to come.

I have served on many juries in every facet of our business, and I am thoroughly convinced that the Society of Illustrators Annual Exhibitions are run with impeccable fairness and without bias.

Whether you have ever won a medal or not, being included in any Society Annual is a great honor, and the 39th Annual is surely no exception. Our jury this year included the best talent there is, and they were very selective. Congratulations to all who have work in this volume.

I wish to extend my appreciation and special thanks to Murry Tinkelman, my Assistant Chairman, and Anita Kunz, D.J. Stout, Bill Mayer, John Rush, all the jury chairpersons, Terry Brown and the wonderful Society staff, Vincent DiFate, and last but not least, all of you out there who work very hard to make your mark in the unique field of American illustration.

The Society of Illustrators has been, and always will be, there for you. Come join us and make history into the next century.

Wendell Minor
Chairman, 39th Annual Exhibition

Illustrators Hall of Fame

Since 1958, the Society of Illustrators has elected to its Hall of Fame artists recognized for their "distinguished achievement in the art of illustration." The list of previous winners is truly a "Who's Who" of illustration. Former Presidents of the Society meet annually to elect those who will be so honored.

Hall of Fame Committee 1997

Chairman	Murray Tinkelman
Chairman Emeritus	Willis Pyle
Former Presidents	Diane Dillon
	Peter Fiore
	Charles McVicker
	Wendell Minor
	Howard Munce
	Alvin J. Pimsler
	Warren Rogers
	Eileen Hedy Schultz
	Shannon Stirnweis
	David K. Stone
	John Witt

Hall of Fame Laureates 1997

Leo & Diane Dillon
Frank McCarthy
Chesley Bonestell
Joe DeMers
Maynard Dixon
Harrison Fisher

Hall of Fame Laureates 1958-1996

1958	Norman Rockwell
1959	Dean Cornwell
1959	Harold Von Schmidt
1960	Fred Cooper
1961	Floyd Davis
1962	Edward Wilson
1963	Walter Biggs
1964	Arthur William Brown
1965	Al Parker
1966	Al Dorne
1967	Robert Fawcett
1968	Peter Helck
1969	Austin Briggs
1970	Rube Goldberg
1971	Stevan Dohanos
1972	Ray Prohaska
1973	Jon Whitcomb
1974	Tom Lovell
1974	Charles Dana Gibson*
1974	N.C. Wyeth*
1975	Bernie Fuchs
1975	Maxfield Parrish*
1975	Howard Pyle*
1976	John Falter
1976	Winslow Homer*
1976	Harvey Dunn*
1977	Robert Peak
1977	Wallace Morgan*
1977	J.C. Leyendecker*
1978	Coby Whitmore

1978	Norman Price*	1989	Erté
1978	Frederic Remington*	1989	John Held Jr.*
1979	Ben Stahl	1989	Arthur Ignatius Keller*
1979	Edwin Austin Abbey*	1990	Burt Silverman
1979	Lorraine Fox*	1990	Robert Riggs*
1980	Saul Tepper	1990	Morton Roberts*
1980	Howard Chandler Christy*	1991	Donald Teague
1980	James Montgomery Flagg*	1991	Jessie Willcox Smith*
1981	Stan Galli	1991	William A. Smith*
1981	Frederic R. Gruger*	1992	Joe Bowler
1981	John Gannam*	1992	Edwin A. Georgi*
1982	John Clymer	1992	Dorothy Hood*
1982	Henry P. Raleigh*	1993	Robert McGinnis
1982	Eric (Carl Erickson)*	1993	Thomas Nast*
1983	Mark English	1993	Coles Phillips*
1983	Noel Sickles*	1994	Harry Anderson
1983	Franklin Booth*	1994	Elizabeth Shippen Green*
1984	Neysa Moran McMein*	1994	Ben Shahn*
1984	John LaGatta*	1995	James Avati
1984	James Williamson*	1995	McClelland Barclay*
1985	Charles Marion Russell*	1995	Joseph Clement Coll*
1985	Arthur Burdett Frost*	1995	Frank E. Schoonover*
1985	Robert Weaver	1996	Herb Tauss
1986	Rockwell Kent*	1996	Anton Otto Fischer*
1986	Al Hirschfeld	1996	Winsor McCay*
1987	Haddon Sundblom*	1996	Violet Oakley*
1987	Maurice Sendak	1996	Mead Schaeffer*
1988	René Bouché*		
1988	Pruett Carter*		
1988	Robert T. McCall		

Presented Posthumosly

Hall of Fame 1997
Leo & Diane Dillon b. 1933

Leo Dillon and Diane Sober were born in March 1933—eleven days apart. Leo was born in Brooklyn, New York, and Diane just outside of Los Angeles, California. Each of them began drawing pictures as young children, and when they met at Parsons School of Design in New York in 1954, they were both single-minded in their mutual dedication to a life of art. They were fiercely competitive, or as Leo says, "This wasn't mere competition, it was war. We spent a lot of time and energy trying to prove ourselves to each other. In the midst of all this, born of mutual recognition of our respective strengths, we fell in love."

In 1956 the Dillons graduated from Parsons and in 1957 they decided to be married. Leo worked as an art director for a men's magazine, and Diane had a position in an advertising agency, but they soon made the next most important decision of their creative lives. They quit their jobs and started a Design Studio at home called simply, Studio 2.

As freelance artists their work included advertising, book covers, album covers, movie posters, and magazine illustration. Happily, they discovered the world of fantasy and science fiction and slowly they began to build a substantial client list. Though they were working more, they were barely making a living and life was hard. But they never lost the passion for their work or their dedication that kept them constantly searching for excellence. Their greatest strength was the enormity of their combined talent. It encompassed their shared passion for ancient Egypt, the Renaissance, Folklore from all over the world and of course, Art Deco. Added to their extraordinary technical skill and an imagination fueled by two very separate sensibilities, they were able to produce work that had a broad range of style and diversity unique in their field. For their extraordinary accomplishment they received recognition in 1971 by the International Science Fiction Association in the form of the Hugo Award, followed in 1982 by the Balrog Award for a Lifetime Contribution to Science Fiction/Fantasy Art.

One day, one of their book covers caught the attention of an editor at Dial Press, and for the first time the Dillons found themselves illustrating a picture book, *The Ring in the Prairie: A Shawnee Tale*, published in 1970. It was the beginning of a whole new direction for them and they embraced it with joy. Only six years later they would complete *Why Mosquitoes Buzz in People's Ears: A West African Tale*, that would receive the 1977 Caldecott Award for the best illustrated children's picture book, awarded annually by the American Library Association.

For Leo this was a major event as he was the first African American to win a Caldecott Medal. The very next year they were awarded a second Caldecott for *Ashanti To Zulu: African Traditions*. This time they became the first illustrators to ever win consecutive Caldecott Medals.

They continued exploring new techniques and media, new cultures and traditions, and always with impeccable research and a passion for perfection. They have deliberately chosen books that give children a sense of pride in themselves, and fire their imagination, and African American culture and history has become a cornerstone of their work.

Intriguingly, the Dillons work together on the same piece of artwork, passing it back and forth with the end result a perfect marriage of skills. They credit the existence of a "third artist" who emerges as each of them works on an image. A line can be started by one and finished by the other, and the composition evolves as the work continues back and forth. Both Leo and Diane believe in the magical element of it all—together they create a picture that neither one of them could have created alone.

Although their greatest joy is to be in the middle of the "next book," they have also been teachers and lecturers and their work is exhibited widely across the country and abroad. They taught at the School of Visual Arts from 1969 to 1977 and were awarded Honorary Doctorates at Parsons in 1991. They received the Society of Illustrators Hamilton King Award in 1997 and Diane served as the Society's first woman President from 1987 to 1989.

Leo and Diane continue to live in their brownstone in the Cobble Hill section of Brooklyn with their son Lee Dillon, a talented painter and sculptor. In fact, Lee may well be the silent "fourth artist" as he too has collaborated on occasional projects.

Their awards and honors are innumerable, among them: New York Times Best Illustrated Awards, the Boston Globe Horn Book awards, Coretta Scott King Award and Honor, a Gold Medal from the Society of Illustrators as well as thirty Certificates of Merit, and four from the Art Directors Club of New York, and two Library of Congress Annual Listings. Perhaps the most recent is truly an indication that this indominable pair continue in their search for excellence and truth. In 1996 Leo and Diane Dillon were the recipients of the prestigious Hans Christian Andersen Award.

Dilys Evans

Her Stories — African-American Folktales and Fairy Tales and True Tales
told by Virginia Hamilton, Blue Sky Press, 1995, acrylic on Bainbridge Board.

Like many illustrators of his era, young Frank McCarthy was enthralled by the adventurous, courageous exploits of Prince Valiant, Flash Gordon, and the characters N.C. Wyeth brought to life—so much so that the walls of his boyhood tree houses were covered with copies he'd drawn of the beloved illustrations. This early fascination with daring, athletic heroes has carried through his dual-career life. McCarthy was not only a prolific illustrator of paperback covers, magazine stories, and major advertising for films from the 1940s through the late 1960s, he also became an outstanding fine arts Western painter from the end of the '60s to the present.

Born in 1924 in New York City, McCarthy drew pictures throughout his grade school years in Scarsdale, New York. As a teenager, he ventured into Manhattan to study during the summer at the Art Students League under George Bridgman, the author of many anatomy books, who gave him a strong appreciation for the dynamic human form. He was later a student of Reginald Marsh, a well-known painter of the Depression Era. Pratt Institute followed high school, where, McCarthy modestly claims, "I was by far not the best student--but somehow I managed to muddle through." During that time he attended many fascinating and edifying lectures at the Society of Illustrators by great artists such as John Gannam, Al Parker, and Harold Von Schmidt.

Soon after graduation, McCarthy worked as an apprentice at Illustrators Incorporated, where he wrapped packages, made deliveries, and assembled mechanicals. Once he became a staff artist he worked on many *Saturday Evening Post* ads for which he had to retouch his own veloxes. This task required fastidious attention to pattern, value, and contrast, which was to become a well-respected and sought after hallmark of his work.

The artist went freelance in 1946 (his first job earned him $7.50). In the early '50s he joined Fredman Studio, which would later become the Fredman Chaite Studios. His reputation began to grow as that of a talented illustrator of both paperback covers and magazine stories—especially those with Western, action-oriented, or as McCarthy puts it, "shoot 'em up bang bang" themes.

While producing for magazines, such as *Collier's, Outdoor Life, Redbook, True,* and publishers, including Avon, Dell, and Fawcett, McCarthy developed his trademark skills. He possessed an adept control of color values and contrasts which reproduced extremely well. He also had an ability to conceive and execute scenes at the climax of action and drama, whether it be two cowboys with their guns drawn, or Native American warriors charging into battle. And he was not solely concerned with the action. McCarthy enhanced it by placing his figures within the grandeur of stunning American landscapes—red-rocked canyons, sage brush deserts, snow covered mountain ranges. During his busiest periods, McCarthy painted up to four book covers a month.

In the 1960s film studios took advantage of the fact that illustrators, rather than photographers, could often better dramatize a story's plot, themes, and characters in one coherent, compelling image. "There was no one better than Frank McCarthy for the action movies," remarks illustration historian Walt Reed. "Anything they couldn't photograph, they'd have me paint," recalls McCarthy. He flourished as an illustrator of advertising imagery (including posters, record cover art and the like) for major movie studios like Paramount, United Artists, Universal, and Warner Brothers. He painted many movie stars--almost always from film stills--including John Wayne in "The Green Berets," Sean Connery in "Thunderball," Charlton Heston in "The Ten Commandments," and James Garner in "The Great Escape."

McCarthy remembers a particularly challenging job during this busy time: creating the recognizable likenesses of Tony Curtis and Yul Brynner as they battled each other with swords while on horseback. "It's hard to do because when two guys are fighting, their faces don't look the same as they do in everyday life. And they were in profile, not head on." Numerous versions later, the image for "Taras Bulba" was completed for United Artists.

In 1968 McCarthy began to move away from commercial illustration when Charlie Dorsa, a good friend from his first studio job, propelled him into the world of Western fine art. Dorsa introduced him to a sales person at a gallery who, upon seeing McCarthy's paperback covers, remarked, "If you can do that for me, I can sell them."

McCarthy took him up on the offer and within just a few years he stopped doing commercial work and devoted himself exclusively to painting Western art for galleries nationwide. Today he continues with this passion, conveniently based in glorious Sedona, Arizona, an area rich in history and inspiration for his Western themes.

Clare McLean

"The Train," movie poster for United Artists featuring Burt Lancaster.

Hall of Fame 1997
Chesley Bonestell (1888 - 1986)

I never met Chesley Bonestell, although his painting of the newly-formed moon rising above a lava sea on ancient earth is one of my earliest and most vivid memories of illustrative art. The painting appeared in the first installment of a remarkable series that ran in *Life* magazine entitled, "The World We Live In," and for a boy whose mind was full of wonder about such things, what a vision it was. It appeared in December of 1952; I was seven then, and it changed my life forever. Remarkably, Bonestell was just weeks away from his sixty-fifth birthday and only eight years into his career as an astronomical illustrator: a career that would ultimately garner him an international reputation and enduring fame. But Chesley Bonestell had pursued three distinct careers over the course of his long life, and in each had left an abiding mark on the twentieth century.

A native Californian, Bonestell's young life was besieged by tragedy. His mother died of pneumonia before his first birthday, and in 1906 he and his family narrowly escaped death when the San Francisco earthquake destroyed their home. In the following year he moved to New York to attend the Columbia University School of Architecture but left in 1910, never to complete his studies. Over the next three decades he worked primarily as an architectural designer and renderer for such prestigious firms as Willis Polk and William Van Alen. The Van Alen firm is especially noted for having designed one of America's great tributes to art deco, New York City's Chrysler Building. Bonestell's many design aspects for the building include the gleaming silver needle and baleful gargoyles atop the famous structure. Other notable structures in which Bonestell had a hand include the Sherry-Netherland Hotel at Central Park, the U.S. Supreme Court Building in Washington D.C., and San Francisco's Golden Gate Bridge.

In 1938, with World War II imminent and with construction at a virtual standstill, Bonestell turned to Hollywood where his considerable artistic abilities quickly transformed him into one of the most sought after and highly paid matte painters in the film industry. Many of the interior and exterior views of the cathedral in the 1939 version of "The Hunchback of Notre Dame" with Charles Laughton, were actually paintings produced by Bonestell to recreate that famous structure as it appeared in the 15th century. The fabulous Xanadu of Orson Welles' 1941 cinematic opus "Citizen Kane," existed nowhere beyond the few single-story sets built on the RKO lot and in a series of exquisitely convincing works that Bonestell painted on glass

The artist, circa 1958

for the production. Other classic films in which his art appeared include, "How Green Was My Valley" (1941), "The Magnificent Ambersons" (1942), "The Horn Blows at Midnight" (1945), "Rhapsody in Blue" (1945), and "The Fountainhead" (1949). In 1949, at the suggestion of legendary science fiction author Robert A. Heinlein, Bonestell was introduced to film producer George Pal and thus began an affiliation that included such classic SF movies as "Destination Moon" (1950), "When Worlds Collide" (1951), "The War of the Worlds" (1953), and the Conquest of Space" (1955). "Destination Moon" is widely acknowledged by film historians as the catalyst that ignited the highly successful SF movie boom of the 1950s.

In 1944, while in the thick of his Hollywood involvement, Bonestell made an unsolicited submission to *Life* of a series of paintings of the planet Saturn as viewed from five of its moons, thus exercising his lifelong avocation for astronomy. The works, stunningly majestic and authoritatively detailed, appeared in the May 29, 1944, issue. For many readers who had never seen such subjects so convincingly portrayed, the far flung worlds of the solar system were transformed into places which suddenly seemed real and accessible. Additional, similar works for articles in *Life Look*, *Coronet*, and elsewhere, and book collaborations over the next four decades with such astronomy and rocketry experts as Willy Ley, Wernher von Braun, Arthur C. Clarke, and Dr. Robert Richardson, helped to persuade the American public of both the desirability and practicality of space travel. In those halcyon days when America earnestly believed that it could attain any goal for which it reached, Bonestell was the unequivocal "dean" of astronomical artists and a man of celebrity status in the illustration community.

In 1986, three months prior to Bonestell's death at the age of ninety-eight, Dr. Carl Sagan identified asteroid (3129) 1979MK2 as "Bonestell" in recognition of the artist's profound influence on popular interest in the heavens. In a subsequent newspaper interview, and with an apparently characteristic acerbic wit, Bonestell referred to his late friend, rocketry pioneer Willy Ley, who some years earlier had had a lunar crater named in his honor. "An asteroid is a flying mountain," Bonestell declared. "I go around the sun. Willy doesn't move."

Vincent DiFate
President, Society of Illustrators

"Saturn from Mimas," 1943. The second largest planet in our solar system, Saturn rises majestically over the horizon of Mimas, one of its tiny inner moons. Art courtesy of Bonestell Space Art.

Hall of Fame 1997
Joe DeMers (1910-1984)

A man of great personal charm and warmth, Joseph Albert DeMers was also blessed with exquisite taste, which was reflected in his illustrations, his gallery paintings and later, in his art and antiques gallery on Hilton Head Island.

A native of San Diego, California, DeMers' artistic and entrepreneurial talents became apparent at a very young age. Not only did he start painting when he was five years old, but soon thereafter began selling his art door to door out of his bicycle basket. While still a youngster he painted scenes on bass drums for traveling bands and on spare-tire covers in order to support himself. He went on to study art in 1929 at the Fine Arts Galleries in San Diego, and a year later received a scholarship to the Chouinard Art Institute in Los Angeles, which he attended for three-and-a-half years. He studied under Pruett Carter and later became an instructor there, teaching classes in "Theory and Use of Color," "Abstract Design and Composition in Relation to Illustration," and "Landscape Painting." He received additional scholarships from Chouinard and for another nine years continued to study there in the evenings.

By the time he was 23, DeMers was exhibiting in galleries and getting extremely good notices from art critics throughout the country. However, those were the years of the 1930s Depression— good reviews didn't mean big bucks. DeMers knew some people in the motion picture industry so, after a prestigious but low-paying job of helping design the 1935 Worlds Fair in San Diego, he turned to Hollywood and began working as a production designer, visual consultant and illustrator for Warner Bothers, later doing some of the same kind of work for their big cross-town rival, Metro-Goldwyn-Mayer. Although DeMers didn't consider this the high point of his career, he nevertheless enjoyed working with a young director in the late 1930s on a picture still acclaimed a masterpiece. The director was John Huston and the film was "The Maltese Falcon." Among other films that DeMers worked on were "Arsenic and Old Lace," "Angels with Dirty Faces," and "Sergeant York."

But the Hollywood life style paled after awhile, so DeMers ventured into the publishing business. With a couple of partners, he decided that 1945 was the time to get into the children's book arena. There were virtually no book publishers in the children's field who were turning out relatively inexpensive books. He achieved a modicum of success, with four best-selling books which he wrote and illustrated, but soon after the war the big publishing houses began moving into the field and DeMers' company was simply not big enough to compete.

His first editorial assignment came from *Fortune* magazine—to illustrate "Ham and Eggs" for an article on "fast food" restaurants along the California coast. *Esquire* magazine followed with a five year contract to do the "Esquire Girls," an arrangement from which DeMers managed to extricate himself after 18 months.

In the late 1940s DeMers began getting story illustration assignments from some of the national magazines. He moved to the East Coast and joined the Charles E. Cooper Studio in New York where many of the "stars" of that period were working. DeMers' great flair for style and brilliant use of color, loosely painted, soon caught the attention of more art directors. His delightful illustrations portraying chic women amid tasteful backgrounds began appearing in popular magazines such as *McCall's, Cosmopolitan, The Ladies' Home Journal, Good Housekeeping* and *The Saturday Evening Post*. He also found a steady market abroad, where his work appeared in such European publications as *Paris Match, Jour de France* and *Marie Clair*. Aside from his editorial illustrations, DeMers also worked on such national advertising campaigns as Jello, Pepsi-Cola, Life Savers, Philip Morris, and many others.

In 1969 DeMers, with his wife Janice and daughter Danielle, moved to Hilton Head Island, South Carolina, where two other members of the Society of Illustrators Hall of Fame, Joe Bowler and Coby Whitmore, also resided. Within two years DeMers had opened a gallery in Harbour Town, filled it with antiques, objets d'art and interesting paintings, and just as his illustrations showcased his unique, excellent taste, so did the gallery. Upstairs, he built a studio for himself so that his penchant for painting could be fulfilled when the spirit moved him.

DeMers' paintings have hung in many major American galleries, including the Museum of Modern Art in New York City, the Corcoran Gallery in Washington, D.C. and The Palace of the Legion of Honor in San Francisco.

Arpi Ermoyan

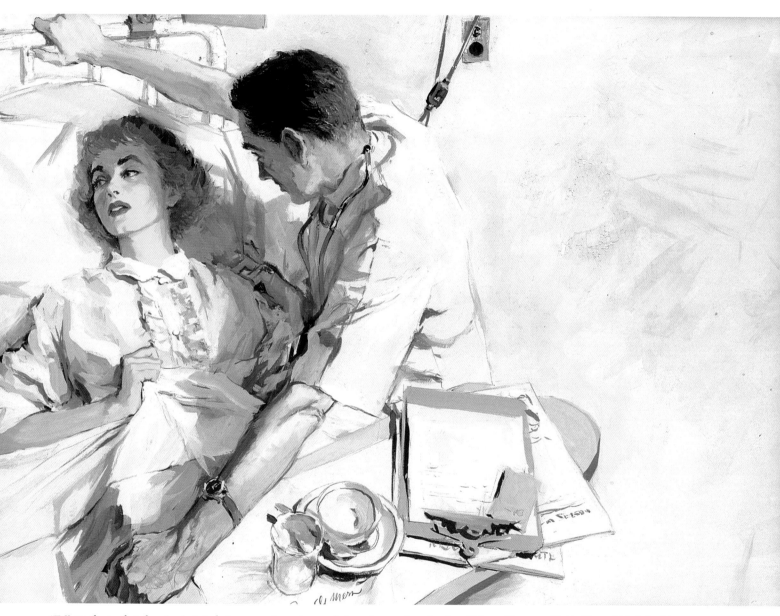

"Tell me the truth," she pleaded, "what are people saying—what are they saying about me?" from "Sweetest Girl in Town," *McCall's*, May 1953.
Permanent Collection of the Society of Illustrators Museum of American Illustration.

Hall of Fame 1997
Maynard Dixon (1875-1946)

Maynard Dixon came into my life in 1974. At that time I was spending my summers painting landscapes in northern New Mexico and studying the rich art history of the region. Discovering my first Dixon painting at Forrest Fenn's Gallery in Santa Fe was a seminal experience. Maynard Dixon's clarity of light, form, and composition were as pure as that found in Edward Hopper's and Rockwell Kent's work.

Why had I not known of Dixon's work before? I have since learned that many artists and illustrators who made a reputation for themselves west of the Mississippi have been historically less prominent on the national scene. But Dixon's reputation as one of the best artist/illustrators of his day continues to grow and expand beyond his time and beyond the Mississippi; east to national, and international renown.

Born in Fresno, California, Maynard knew at a very early age that he wanted to be an illustrator of the Old West. He loved the work of Howard Pyle, A. B. Frost, and Frederic Remington. In 1891, at the age of sixteen, he sent two sketch books to Remington hoping for some advice. Dixon was not disappointed. Remington liked what he saw in the young artist's work and encouraged him to "draw, draw, draw and always from nature."

Dixon's first illustrations appeared in *The Overland Monthly* in 1893. He was only eighteen years old then, three years younger than N.C. Wyeth was when his first illustration was published on the cover of *The Saturday Evening Post* in 1903. In San Francisco, Dixon's career flourised with numerous assignments for the *San Francisco Morning Call*.

The famous editor, Charles F. Lummis, became a great supporter, mentor and friend to the young artist. Writers like Jack London began requesting his work, and in 1900 Dixon illustrated the frontispiece for London's first book, *Son of the Wolf*, published by Houghton Mifflin Company.

Dixon's studio was destroyed in the earthquake of 1906. This event proved to be a catalyst for relocation to New York in 1907 where the artist refined his illustration skills in such famous publications as *Scribner's*, *Outdoor Life*, *Collier's* and *McClure's*. Maynard's fame grew with the publication of Clarence Mulford's *Hopalong Cassidy* book series from 1910 to 1913. He was elected to membership in the New York Society of Illustrators in 1911, and in 1912 had several paintings accepted in the National Academy of Design's annual exhibition.

The West proved to be such a powerful force in Maynard's life that his stay in the East was relatively short. He returned to San Francisco in 1912 and opened what became his famous studio at 728 Montgomery Street (the building is now registered as a national landmark). It is interesting to note that the building sustained damage in the earthquake of 1989, and is currently unoccupied.

Dixon's second marriage to the photographer Dorothea Lange in 1920 also proved to be a pivotal event in his life. Although he continued to create poster designs, and illustrate for companies such as Standard Oil and Southern Pacific through the '20s and '30s, Lange encouraged Dixon to focus more on his personal work. He never forgot Remington's advice. Working from life on painting and sketching trips, he developed an illustration style that translated beautifully into an approach to painting that was unique.

His last major book project was to do seventy pen-and-ink drawings and watercolors for Francis Parkman's *The Oregon Trail* in 1943. It is one of his finest illustration efforts.

Like Winslow Homer before him and Edward Hopper after, Dixon evolved into one of the finest painters of his time. Today, Dixon's work shines forth with a true grit honesty and a beacon of clarity that renders it timeless.

We owe a great debt to those who believed in Dixon's legacy, for there are many whose flame dies out in the rush for tomorrow. His sons Dan and John Dixon, Dorothea Lange, Edith Hamlin and finally his biographer, Donald J. Hagerty (*Desert Dreams: The Art and Life of Maynard Dixon*) have kept Maynard Dixon's flame burning bright. Through his illustations and paintings Dixon created an image of the West without the Myth, and that is his greatest gift to art and American culture.

In 1993, I was commissioned by Simon and Schuster to design a cover for Larry McMurtry's Streets of Loredo. My design incorporated Maynard Dixon's painting *Cloud World*, and needless to say, the result was a great success. Thanks, Maynard.

Wendell Minor
Past President, Society of Illustrators 1989-1991
Hall of Fame Committee

"The Apache Trail" for Southern Pacific Lines, 1927.

Hall of Fame 1997
Harrison Fisher (1875-1934)

Harrison Fisher was in that exalted company of artists who could draw and paint prototypical American beauties.

Better than any other enticement, magazine publishers found a beautiful woman on the cover would greatly boost newsstand sales. Artists who could provide these beauties with the greatest appeal found quick fame and all the magazines vied for their services. Through this display case, these specialized artists had an extraordinary influence in setting styles with enthusiastic partisan viewers who adopted the hair styles, make-up, and dress presented in the pictures. Fan clubs members corresponded with the artists and among themselves and served as a valuable barometer of popularity to the publishers. Amateur artist admirers regularly copied the cover girls of Gibson, Fisher and others (along with the signatures and many of these efforts still survive, causing some confusion with today's collectors).

For several years Fisher played no favorites between *The Saturday Evening Post, The Associated Sunday Magazine, Life, Collier's Weekly, The Ladies' Home Journal, Hearst's International,* and *Cosmopolitan.* After the latter two magazines combined, Fisher was signed to a long-term, exclusive contract to do all their covers. This did not prevent him, however, from also extensively marketing his pictures as frameable reproductions and post cards through the Cosmopolitan Print Department where they outsold works by all of the other artists. There were also the many gift books which were periodically assembled and published, presenting his latest collections of femme fatales. This all added up to making him a very rich artist with an income of over $75,000 a year (this in 1914).

Despite his success in depicting women and being surrounded by beautiful models, Fisher never married, claiming to be "too busy." Over the years he produced so many Cover Girls that even he confessed that he'd had enough and "would prefer to do an occasional sea lion or a cow."

Fisher was always a good candidate for feature interviews about "What makes a Woman Beautiful" and gamely gave advice to aspiring models recommending good character from within rather than a reliance on cosmetics. (Probably not what they wanted to hear!) It was the types of models Fisher presented that gave them their popularity— patrician, poised, upper-class, with a demure femininity in accord with the social ideals of pre-World War I society.

Fisher's career continued on into the '20s when he had to accommodate his norms of beauty and dress to the era of bobbed hair, cloche hats and a generation of unabashed man-hunters. However, his new women held their own against the Russell Patterson and John Held Jr. flappers and still continued to carry their Harrison Fisher air of class.

Fisher came by all this popular and financial success by paying his dues early on. The son of a landscape painter, Hujgo Antoine Fisher, he was born in Brooklyn, New York. Because he was a sickly child, his family moved to the more temperate climate of Lameda, California, when he was six. Following the encouragement and tutelage of his father, he attended classes at the Mark Hopkins Institute of Art. His first professional art job was on the staff of the *San Francisco Call;* later he worked for the *Examiner.* In 1898 he transferred to a New York newspaper as a base to try to launch a magazine career. Eventually, *Puck* magazine bought two of his drawings, and he was commissioned to do a cover for *Beverly of Graustark,* a novel that became popular. The pretty girl he painted was also very successful and led to more such assignments. Eventually, the Fisher Girl joined the pantheon of her famous sisters, the "Gibson Girl," the "Christy Girl," and the Coles Phillips "Fadeaway Girl." She has continued to be as alluring today, with an active Harrison Fisher Society, and eager collectors who prize her in any of her myriad manifestations.

Walt Reed
Illustration House

"Couple at the Piano," 1910. Permanent Collection of the Society of Illustrators Museum of American Illustration.

The Hamilton King Award and Special Awards

The Hamilton King Award, created by Mrs. Hamilton King in memory of her husband through a bequest, is presented annually for the best illustration of the year by a member of the Society. The selection is made by former recipients of this award and may be won only once.

Also, the Society of Illustrators presents Special Awards each year for substantial contributions to the profession. The Dean Cornwell Recognition Award honors someone for past service which has proven to have been an important contribution to the Society. The Arthur William Brown Achievement Award honors someone who has made a substantial contribution to the Society over a period of time.

HAMILTON KING AWARD 1965-1997

Year	Recipient	Year	Recipient	Year	Recipient
1965	Paul Calle	1977	Leo & Diane Dillon	1988	James McMullan
1966	Bernie Fuchs	1978	Daniel Schwartz	1989	Guy Billout
1967	Mark English	1979	William Teason	1990	Edward Sorel
1968	Robert Peak	1980	Wilson McLean	1991	Brad Holland
1969	Alan E. Cober	1981	Gerald McConnell	1992	Gary Kelley
1970	Ray Ameijide	1982	Robert Heindel	1993	Jerry Pinkney
1971	Miriam Schottland	1983	Robert M. Cunningham	1994	John Collier
1972	Charles Santore	1984	Braldt Bralds	1995	C.F. Payne
1973	Dave Blossom	1985	Attila Hejja	1996	Etienne Delessert
1974	Fred Otnes	1986	Doug Johnson	1997	Marshall Arisman
1975	Carol Anthony	1987	Kinuko Y. Craft		
1976	Judith Jampel				

Special Awards 1997

Arthur William Brown Achievement Award
Everett Raymond Kinstler

The kind of phone call often received at the Society--and the one often answered with a snicker—is the one from the high-fallutin' curator who asks, "I have a copy of Cosmopolitan Magazine from May 1932, and on page 45 is an illustration. Where is the original?" It would be surprising indeed if five percent of all of the art created for commerce in this century still exists. So when a collection is saved from the dumpster, the Society takes note and there is an award to be bestowed.

Since 1979, Everett Raymond Kinstler has donated over 90 works by nine artists to the Permanent Collection of the Society of Illustrators Museum of American Illustration. Within that assembly are 73 works by Hall of Famer James Montgomery Flagg. This has made the Society's collection synonymous with the pen-and-ink story illustrator and "I Want You" poster delineator who was famous during the first half of this century.

In the twilight of his career, his eyesight failing, Monty turned down a commission to do a portrait but recommended a young buck named Everett Raymond Kinstler for the job. That stroke of luck changed the career of the young illustrator, who had been toiling in the trenches of the comic book and pulp magazine markets, visualizing such heroes as Tarzan, Doc Savage, Hawkman, and Zorro.

Kinstler's career shift has resulted in five Presidential portraits, including the official White House portraits of Gerald Ford and Ronald Reagan; 40-plus Cabinet officers, Supreme Court Justices; stage and film stars; authors, and other celebrities. Ray has been called friend to such luminaries as James Cagney, John Wayne, Tom Wolfe and even Best Man to Tony Bennett.

Beyond his art, Ray's participation in every important arts club in New York, including the National Arts Club, the National Academy, the Players Club, the Lotos Club, and the Century Association, attests to the respect with which he is held. His authorship of several books on painting will pass along the teachings of Frank Vincent DuMond, Ray's most influential teacher at the Art Students League. And his most generous donations of works to the Society's collection, especially those of James Montgomery Flagg, will secure for the future a look at the original art created for publication by one of the best illustrators of his day.

So, when that curator calls about Cosmo '32, page 45--if it's a Flagg, we probably have it.

Terrence Brown
Director, Society of Illustrators

Dean Cornwell Recognition Award
Wallace Morgan

Portrait by William Oberhardt

I didn't know Wallace Morgan (1873-1948) deeper than a long-ago hand shake at the Society's bar, but I did know of the prowess of the hand that wrote his drawings with an individuality that employed no mechanical aids, tricky techniques, special materials, or dependency upon fad.

He left an enviable reputation behind because of the high esteem in which his work was held and because of his fine fellowship, which all published accounts of his life refer to, and because of the important role he played in the fate of the Society. He was a prime mover in the chancy decision to move from 24th Street to the present building, and he presided over the Society for seven years as its president. In World War I, given the rank of Captain, he served as Official Artist with the American Expeditionary Forces. His on-the-spot wartime sketches are an informative joy to study. Many of them reside in the Library of Congress.

Back in 1905 he had a spectacular success with a Sunday feature cloyingly titled, "Fluffy Ruffles," a period he blushingly wished to suppress despite its popularity. Fortunately, however, it brought his work to the attention of magazine editors. From that time until the bleak forties, when editorial fashion obsoleted him, he was a regular in many magazines of the day.

Perhaps the best way to do justice to him is to quote the stern, no-nonsense old giant, Harvey Dunn, from his remarks in the Bulletin at Wally's death in 1948:

> Every artist in the country must acknowledge the stature of Wallace Morgan in the work he did and what he stood for.
>
> Whatever his subject matter, he always saw it with a fresh eye, whether it was Paris, New York or Monhegan Island or the race track, the Deep South, the Fluffy Ruffles or the stuffed shirt. His kindly humor touched them all.
>
> We have lost a great artist, but he has left a great record. His quiet adherence to the things in art that he believed in was the measure of his greatness, as never for a moment was he moved from it by the fads of the day, none of the isms beguiled him or befooled him.

There can be little to add to such an encomium from such a person, except perhaps to say with a bow to Gertrude Stein that a Morgan drawing is a drawing is a drawing.

Howard Munce
Honorary President

HAMILTON KING AWARD 1997
Marshall Arisman b. 1938

Maintaining a delicate balance between painting (fine art) and illustration is a precarious business at best. In his work, Marshall Arisman has been successful mastering the nuanced shift between reality and ambiguity.

The absence of hierarchy signifies difference. Arisman's strong, sometimes confrontational imagery has for over twenty years suggested there is more to illustration than just story-telling.

With literary theory hovering always in the background, Arisman and the late Robert Weaver made frequent reference to the moments when words are inexpressible and illustration thereby becomes visual essay. On a very high and consistent level Arisman has brought the clarity of journalism and its freedom of discourse to illustration. Working as a pictorial essayist his oeuvre assaults the eye and, at times, inflames the mind.

At this point, painter and illustrator meet and depend on each other with engaging closeness. Content is as necessary to Arisman's work as decoration is to others'. There is no question in my mind that Marshall Arisman is a major force in the field of editorial illustration.

From his sense of being, above all things, an artist, he has derived a lofty purpose for his illustration, neither didactic nor moralistic. The dualism between illustration and painting that exists for others has long ago faded from his memory. He uses the freedom of painting—exploring emotion, picture ideas, concepts of space, light and color—to inspire his illustration. He learns from the painting process, and what he knows he applies to his commercial work, which means doing illustration continues to challenge him and sustain his interest.

What is defined as "commercial" illustration today is far broader than in the past due largely to artists like Marshall who use the editorial medium as an outlet for personal imagery. Young art directors are continually discovering him and mature art directors rediscover him.

In 1964, I appointed Marshall Arisman to the faculty of SVA to teach undergraduate illustration. He was a promising young illustrator then. That he has fulfilled that promise, this award would seem to certify. As a teacher, Marshall is a natural. Not too many years later, I asked him to chair the department. He brought new energy into undergraduate illustration, and it was a pleasure for me to observe students gaining success and new understanding of what they were about. Teaching gives Marshall a platform to explore ideas with students about the reciprocal play between art and life.

Over the years, I have watched Marshall mature as an artist and grow and develop as a teacher. Now he is the chair of the graduate MFA. His view of illustration as visual essay was the rationale that launched his program, which has annually attracted a large pool of applicants from which a limited number is accepted.

Marshall has become one of the most sought after speakers at colleges and universities across the country. At Visual Arts, we regard him as one of our ambassadors, not only to let the larger world know the quality of our faculty, but because in his own personal way he carries forward the message of this our 50th Anniversary year that art has value in its own right, that the process of making art is important to human beings, that it creates a quality of life we do not as a society dare be without.

When I asked Marshall about his reaction to the Hamilton King Award, he didn't give me one of those Oscar-winning thank yous but very forthrightly said how particularly honored he was to be this year's recipient and he emphasized the word *particularly* because he had been chosen by his peers who had previously received the award and of whose work he has been a long-time admirer.

I salute the Society of Illustrators for presenting Marshall Arisman with the Hamilton King Award. By doing so, the Society acknowledges its very important role in legitimizing illustration that is adventuresome, outside the mainstream, and making it acceptable. Organizations, like individual artists, need to work to remain fresh and innovative in their approach to their mandate. This choice seems to confirm the leadership direction the Society has taken.

Silas H. Rhodes
Founder/Chairman of the Board, School of Visual Arts

"Three Strikes and You're Out," *California Lawyer Magazine.*

Executive Officers 1996-1997

Honorary President	**Howard Munce**
President	**Vincent DiFate**
Executive Vice President	**Steven Stroud**
Vice President	**Al Lorenz**
Treasurer	**Richard Berenson**
Associate Treasurer	**Judy Francis**
Secretary	**Dennis Dittrich**

Board of Directors 1996-1997

Advisory	**Shannon Stirnweis**
Annual Exhibition	**Wendell Minor**
Christmas Auction	**Patrick Milbourn**
Christmas Fund	**Peter Fiore**
Community Service	**Judy Francis**
Education	**Tim O'Brien**
	Alvin J. Pimsler (*Honorary*)
Extended Membership	**Eric Fowler**
Finance	**Richard Berenson**
Fund Development	**Lewis Johnson**
Gallery (Hanging)	**Alan Goffman**
Government Service	**Gil Cohen**
	Keith Ferris (*Honorary*)
Graphics	**Richard Berenson**
Hall of Fame	**Murray Tinkelman**
	Willis Pyle (*Emeritus*)
House	**Al Lorenz**
Instruction	**Dale Moyer**
International	**Nancy Hoffmann**
Lecture Series	**Joel Iskowitz**
Legislation	**Jon Weiman**
Life/Senior Membership	**Alvin J. Pimsler**
Membership	**Dennis Dittrich**
Members Gallery	**Mitchell Hooks**
Museum	**John Witt**
Orientation Committee	**Eric Fowler**
	Jonathan Schneider
Permanent Collection	**Doreen Minuto**
	Murray Tinkelman
Publications	**Gerald McConnell**
Public Relations	**Richard Solomon**
	Steven Stroud
Special Events	**Emma Crawford**
Welfare	**Warren Rogers**

39th Annual Exhibition Committee

Chairman	**Wendell Minor**
Assistant Chairman	**Murray Tinkelman**
Poster Illustrator	**Anita Kunz**
Poster Designer	**D.J. Stout**
Gallery (Hanging) Committee	**Alan Goffman**

SI Staff

Director	**Terrence Brown**
Assistant Director	**Phyllis Harvey**
Manager	**Michael Sysyn**
Catering	**Karlton Harris**
Staff and Assistants	**Patrick Arrasmith**
	Allen Douglas
	Anna Lee Fuchs
	Kathleen Hanson
	Ed Hasbrouck
	James Mandela
	Donna Sysyn
	Janet Weithas

Illustrators 39 Annual Book

Editor	**Jill Bossert**
Interior Design	**Harish Patel Design**
Cover Design	**Wendell Minor**
Cover Painting	**Bill Mayer**

THE SOCIETY OF
ILLUSTRATORS
39TH ANNUAL OF
AMERICAN
ILLUSTRATION

ILLUSTRATORS
39

EDITORIAL JURY

CHRIS SPOLLEN, Chair
Illustrator

TERRY ALLEN
Illustrator

RAÚL COLÓN
Illustrator

CHRISTINE CURRY
Illustration Editor
The New Yorker

DEBRA MORTON HOYT
Corporate Art Director
W.W. Norton & Company

ANDREW KNER
Art Director
Print and Scenario

DIANE LUGER
Executive Art Director,
Warner Books

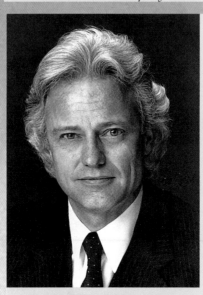

B. MARTIN PEDERSEN
Designer/Publisher
Graphis Press

ATHA TEHON
Associate Publisher/Art Director
Dial Books For Young Readers

EDITORIAL

•••••••••••••••••••••••••••••••••

Award Winners

••••••••••••••••••••••••

BRAD HOLLAND
Gold Medal

C.F. PAYNE
Gold Medal

BRIAN CRONIN
Silver Medal

WILLIAM JOYCE
Silver Medal

GARY KELLEY
Silver Medal

FRANCIS LIVINGSTON
Silver Medal

1

Artist: **BRAD HOLLAND**

Art Director: Al Braverman

Client: New Choices

Medium: Acrylic on Masonite

Size: 18" x 15"

Editorial Gold Medal
BRAD HOLLAND
"Like a lot of artists, I secretly wish the Pope would call some day with a ceiling that needs painting. Doing a picture about stomach problems is less taxing, but this one required an extra rum & Coke to get in the mood. The guy reminds me of an old aunt who used to push herself away from the table saying 'I daresn't have no more.' Then, having made that clear, she'd dive in for seconds."

2

Artist: **C. F. PAYNE**

Art Director: Julie Schrader

Client: Entertainment Weekly

Medium: Mixed

Size: 12" x 7"

Editorial Gold Medal

C.F. PAYNE

"I feel it is an honor not only to receive this award given to me by my peers, but I also appreciate the opportunities the illustration world offers me each day."

E D I T O R I A L ·   *Illustrators* • 39

3

Artist: **BRIAN CRONIN**

Art Director: Judy Garlan

Client: The Atlantic Monthly

Medium: Watercolor, India ink

Size: 11" x 8"

Editorial Silver Medal

BRIAN CRONIN

"I have been working as an illustrator in New York City for the last eleven years. My work appears in various publications both in the U.S. and Europe. At present I am working on a collection of my illustrations for a book and an exhibition at the Irish Museum of Modern Art in Dublin, for the springtime of 1998."

4

Artist: **WILLIAM JOYCE**

Art Director: Françoise Mouly

Client: The New Yorker

Medium: Oil on Bristol board

Size: 14" x 9"

Editorial Silver Medal

WILLIAM JOYCE

The New Yorker called William Joyce requesting that he deliver a finish of a sketch he'd submitted two years earlier—the Macy's Thanksgiving Parade from Hell. Down the avenue you can see the artist's classic "Dinosaur Bob," and Woody, a character that Joyce helped develop for the movie "Toy Story." Without infringing on any Disney copyrights, Joyce nonetheless poked gentle fun at that entertainment conglomerate.

5

Artist: **GARY KELLEY**

Art Director: Lawrence Laukhuf

Client: Angels on Earth

Medium: Pastel on paper

Size: 15" x 14"

Editorial Silver Medal

GARY KELLEY

"I would like to thank George Bellows, Marc Chagall, Paul Colin, Edgar Degas, Edwin Dickinson, Richard Diebenkorn, William Russell Flint, Hal Foster, Juan Gris, Victor Higgins, Per Krogh, Joe Kubert, Tamara de Lempicka, Andrew Loomis, Evsei Moiseyenko, Frederic Remington, Norman Rockwell, Felix Vallotton, Edouard Vuillard, Jerome Witkin, Grant Wood, and N.C. Wyeth, among others, for hleping me expose myself one more year in this marvelous exhibition!"

GARY KELLEY

6
Artist: **FRANCIS LIVINGSTON**
Medium: Oil on board
Size: 24" x 18"

Editorial Silver Medal
FRANCIS LIVINGSTON
"Old movie theatres are almost completely relegated to memory nowadays. The few that remain bring out a nostalgic feeling that most people can relate to immediately. I've painted the Grand Lake from various angles in the past and this is my favorite view. It is not concerned with the activity in the theatre but with the surrounding area instead."

7
Artist: **DUGALD STERMER**
Art Director: Jim MacKenzie
Client: UC Santa Cruz Review Magazine
Medium: Pencil, watercolor on Arches
Size: 14" x 12"

8
Artist: **DAVID O'KEEFE**
Art Director: Kenneth Smith
Client: Time
Medium: Clay sculpture
Size: 10" x 13"

9
Artist: **STEVE BRODNER**
Art Director: Janet Froelich
Client: The New York Times Magazine
Medium: Watercolor
Size: 11" x 11"

10
Artist: **STEVE BRODNER**
Art Directors: Fred Woodward
Gail Anderson
Client: Rolling Stone
Medium: Watercolor on paper
Size: 13" x 9"

11
Artist: **MARK FREDRICKSON**
Art Directors: Arthur Hochstein
Kenneth Smith
Client: Time
Size: 10" x 8"

12
Artist: **PHILIP BURKE**
Art Director: Arthur Hochstein
Client: Time
Medium: Oil on canvas

7

8

9

10

11

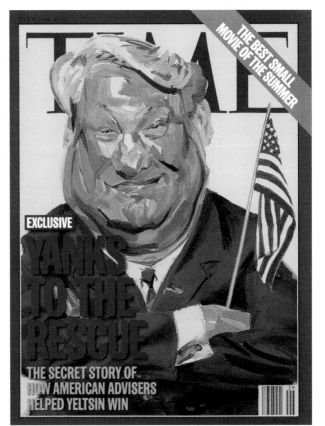

12

13
Artist: **JOE CIARDIELLO**
Art Director: Chris Curry
Client: The New Yorker
Medium: Pen & ink, watercolor

14
Artist: **PHILIP BURKE**
Art Director: Lauren Ramsby
Client: The New York Observer
Medium: Pen & ink, pastel
Size: 10" x 10"

15
Artist: **MARK SUMMERS**
Art Director: Steven Heller
Client: The New York Times
Book Review
Medium: Engraving in scratchboard
Size: 7" x 7"

16
Artist: **MARK SUMMERS**
Art Director: Steven Heller
Client: The New York Times
Book Review
Medium: Engraving in scratchboard
Size: 7" x 6"

17
Artist: **PHILIP BURKE**
Art Director: Lauren Ramsby
Client: The New York Observer
Medium: Oil on canvas
Size: 42" x 56"

18
Artist: **MARK SUMMERS**
Art Director: Steven Heller
Client: The New York Times
Book Review
Medium: Engraving in scratchboard
Size: 5" x 4"

13

14

15

16

17

18

19

Artist: **DREW FRIEDMAN**

Client: The New York Observer

Medium: Watercolor, colored pencil

Size: 7" x 7"

20

Artist: **TIM BORGERT**

Art Director: Lee Walgand

Client: Dayton Daily News

Medium: Watercolor on board

Size: 8" x 11"

21

Artist: **JOHN NICKLE**

Art Director: Betsy Urrico

Client: The Atlantic Monthly

Medium: Acrylic on board

Size: 5" x 4"

22

Artist: **DAVID MOYERS**

Art Director: Bruce Hansen

Client: Playboy

Medium: Acrylic on Bristol board

Size: 7" x 6"

23

Artist: **MIRKO ILIC**

Art Director: Steven Heller

Client: The New York Times

Medium: Computer C-print

Size: 13" x 10"

19

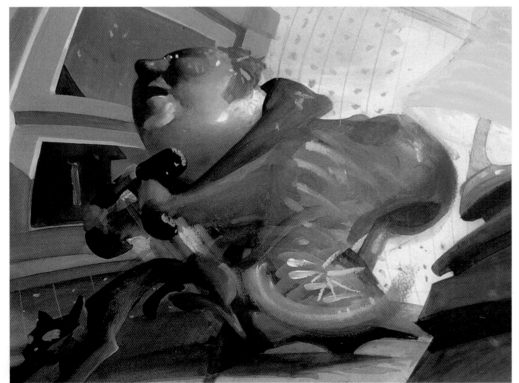

20

21

22

23

24

Artist: **MALCOLM TARLOFSKY**

Art Director: Jane Palecek

Client: Health

Medium: Collage

25

Artist: **C. F. PAYNE**

Art Director: Judy Garlan

Client: The Atlantic Monthly

Medium: Oil, acrylics, watercolor,
      pencils on cold press board

Size: 10" x 17"

26

Artist: **C. F. PAYNE**

Art Director: Brad Jansen

Client: NFL Properties

Medium: Oil, acrylics, watercolor,
      pencils on cold press board

Size: 17" x 13"

27

Artist: **C. F. PAYNE**

Art Director: Janet Froelich

Client: The New York Times Magazine

Medium: Oil, acrylic, watercolor,
      pencils on cold press board

Size: 11" x 10"

24

25

26

27

28
Artist: **BILL MAYER**
Art Director: Anthony Arnold
Client: Slant
Medium: Dyes, gouache
Size: 15" x 11"

29
Artist: **MEL ODOM**
Art Director: Tom Staebler
Client: Playboy
Size: 8" x 6"

30
Artist: **JOHN COLLIER**
Art Director: David Armario
Client: Men's Journal
Medium: Monoprint on acetate
Size: 13" x 10"

31
Artist: **ANITA KUNZ**
Art Director: Arthur Hochstein
Client: Time
Medium: Watercolor, gouache on board
Size: 13" x 9"

32
Artist: **RAFAL OLBINSKI**
Art Director: Arthur Hochstein
Client: Time
Size: 14" x 10"

33
Artist: **ANITA KUNZ**
Art Director: Fred Woodward
Client: Rolling Stone
Medium: Watercolor, collage on board
Size: 12" x 7"

34
Artist: **ANITA KUNZ**
Art Director: Louise Kollenbaum
Client: California Lawyer
Medium: Watercolor, collage on board
Size: 10" x 8"

28

29

30

31

32

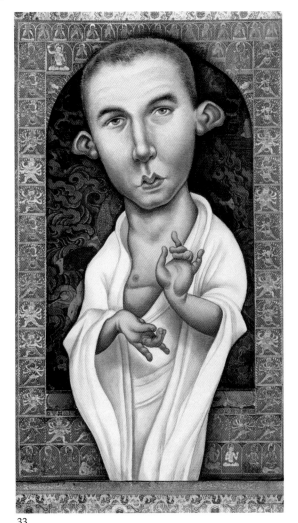

33

34

35
Artist: **JORDIN ISLIP**
Art Director: Jay Johnson
Client: Colorado Cyclist
Medium: Mixed on paper
Size: 16" x 13"

36
Artist: **GREGORY MANCHESS**
Art Director: Rina Migliaccio
Client: Gentlemen's Quarterly
Medium: Oil on gessoed board
Size: 11" x 16"

37
Artist: **MARSHALL ARISMAN**
Art Director: Louise Kollenbaum
Client: California Lawyer
Medium: Oil
Size: 19" x 6"

38
Artist: **JULIAN ALLEN**
Art Director: Janet Froelich
Client: The New York Times Magazine
Medium: Graphite, oil on Bristol
Size: 18" x 14"

39
Artist: **GREGORY MANCHESS**
Art Director: Steve Connaster
Client: Private Clubs
Medium: Oil on gessoed board
Size: 13" x 18"

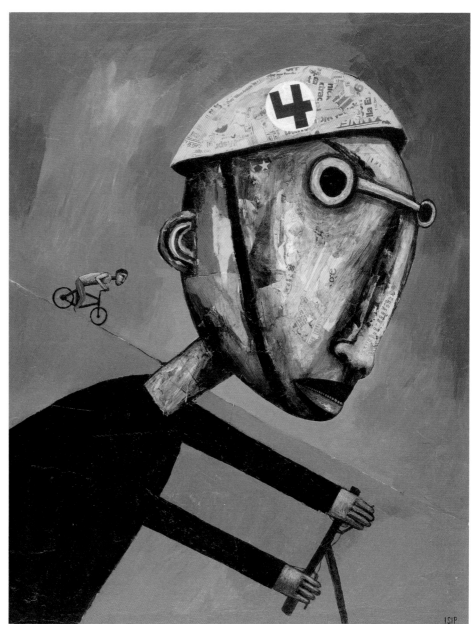

35

36

37

38

39

40
Artist: **MATT MAHURIN**
Art Director: Diana LaGuardia
Client: Esquire
Medium: Digital

41
Artist: **MARIA KALMAN**
Art Director: Judy Garlan
Client: The Atlantic Monthly
Medium: Gouache on paper
Size: 9" x 11"

42
Artist: **MICHAEL BARTALOS**
Art Director: Robert Jensen
Client: Design Quarterly
Medium: Cut paper on board
Size: 15" x 23"

43
Artist: **M. PARASKEVAS**
Art Director: Jamie Easler
Client: United Airlines
Medium: Acrylic on gessoed canvas

44
Artist: **MIKE BENNY**
Art Director: David Herbick
Client: Civilization
Medium: Acrylic
Size: 15" x 16"

40

41

42

43

44

45
Artist: **MICHAEL PLANK**
Art Director: Rick Jost
Client: Discovery magazine
Medium: Oil on canvas
Size: 14" x 13"

46
Artist: **CHRISTOPHER A. KLEIN**
Art Director: Mark Holmes
Client: National Geographic Magazine
Medium: Oil on masonite
Size: 15" x 18"

47
Artist: **JOHN GURCHE**
Art Director: Chris Sloan
Client: National Geographic Society
Medium: Acrylic on gessoed masonite
Size: 10" x 14"

48
Artist: **KATHERINE MAHONEY**
Art Director: Steven Charny
Client: McCall's
Medium: Mixed
Size: 13" x 7"

49
Artist: **BILL MAYER**
Art Director: David Whitmore
Client: Discover Channel Monthly
Medium: Dyes, gouache
Size: 12" x 9"

45

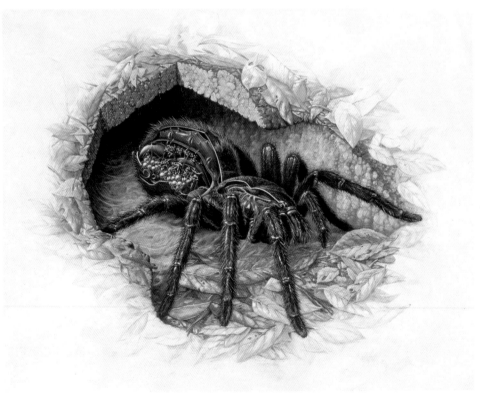

46

47

48

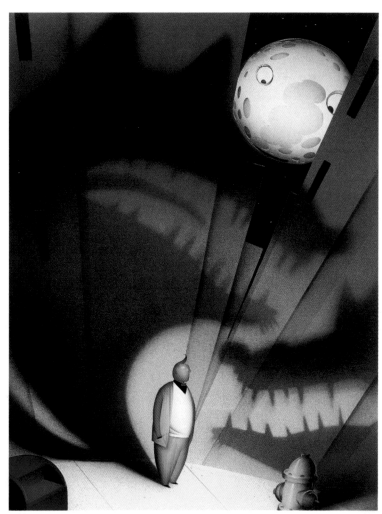

49

50
Artist: **BENÔIT**
Art Director: Susan Casey
Client: Outside
Medium: Oil on paper
Size: 15" x 11"

51
Artist: **MIRKO ILIC**
Art Director: Steven Heller
Client: The New York Times
Medium: Computer C-print
Size: 13" x 10"

52
Artist: **WILSON McLEAN**
Art Director: Kerig Pope
Client: Playboy
Medium: Oil on canvas
Size: 19" x 29"

53
Artist: **BRUCE McCALL**
Art Director: David Harris
Client: Vanity Fair
Medium: Gouache
Size: 14" x 20"

50

51

52

54
Artist: **GARY HEAD**
Art Director: Jeff Capaldi
Client: American Medical News
Medium: Oil on book binding
Size: 13" x 10"

55
Artist: **JODY HEWGILL**
Art Director: Barbara Dow
Client: Eastside Week
Medium: Acrylic on board
Size: 9" x 10"

56
Artist: **JOSEPH DANIEL FIEDLER**
Art Director: Nick Torello
Client: Omni
Medium: Alkyd on Strathmore Bristol

57
Artist: **JOSEPH DANIEL FIEDLER**
Art Director: Steven Heller
Client: The New York Times Book
Review
Medium: Alkyd on Strathmore Bristol
Size: 15" x 14"

58
Artist: **JULIETTE BORDA**
Art Director: Yvonne Duran
Client: Shape Magazine
Medium: Gouache on paper
Size: 11" x 9"

59
Artist: **JULIETTE BORDA**
Art Director: Sandra Schneiders
Client: The Washington Post Magazine
Medium: Gouache on paper
Size: 11" x 9"

54

55

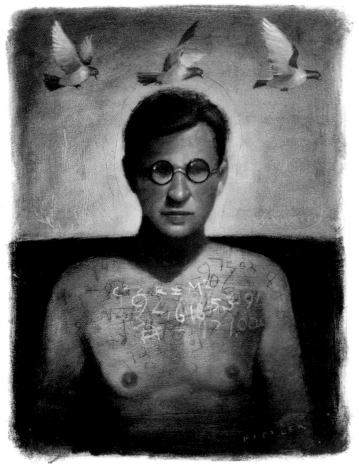

56

57

58

59

60
Artist: **ANA JUAN**
Art Director: Françoise Mouly
Client: The New Yorker
Medium: Acrylic, colored pencil on paper
Size: 18" x 153

61
Artist: **JOHN COLLIER**
Art Director: Louise Kollenbaum
Client: California Lawyer
Medium: Oil, pastel
Size: 24" x 18"

62
Artist: **LORENZO MATTOTTI**
Art Director: Christine Curry
Client: The New Yorker
Medium: Pastel, pencil on paper
Size: 9" x 12"

63
Artist: **STEVE BRODNER**
Art Directors: Fred Woodward
                Gail Anderson
Client: Rolling Stone
Medium: Watercolor

60

61

62

63

64
Artist: **PHIL BOATWRIGHT**
Art Director: J. Porter
Client: Yankee Magazine
Medium: Oil, acrylic, found objects on
Strathmore

65
Artist: **JEFFREY FISHER**
Art Director: Christin Gangi
Client: Meigher Communications

66
Artist: **JAMES BENNETT**
Medium: Oil on board
Size: 19" x 16"

67
Artist: **BRIAN AJHAR**
Art Director: Annie Huang
Client: Bon Appétit Magazine
Medium: Watercolor, ink on watercolor
paper
Size: 14" x 17"

68
Artist: **TOM HERZBERG**
Art Director: Nancy Canfield
Client: Chicago Tribune Magazine
Medium: Watercolor on paper
Size: 12" x 10"

69
Artist: **MELINDA BECK**
Art Director: Melissa Tardiff
Client: The New York Times
Medium: Scratchboard, collage of
painted paper and
old photographs on board
Size: 16" x 13"

64

65

66

67

68

69

70
Artist: **BRIAN CRONIN**
Art Directors: Frank Baseman
Betsy Brecht
Client: Philadelphia Magazine
Medium: Watercolor, pen & ink
Size: 9" x 9"

71
Artist: **BRIAN CRONIN**
Art Director: Ken McFarlin
Client: The New York Times Magazine
Medium: Watercolor, India ink
Size: 10" x 10"

72
Artist: **MARK RYDEN**
Art Director: Cynthia L. Currie
Client: Kiplinger's Personal Finance
Magazine
Medium: Oil on board
Size: 16" x 12"

73
Artist: **CATHLEEN TOELKE**
Art Director: Susan Dazzo
Client: Gentlemen's Quarterly
Medium: Gouache on watercolor board
Size: 17" x 13"

74
Artist: **THOMAS SCIACCA**
Art Director: Tom Staebler
Client: Playboy
Medium: Acrylic on rag board
Size: 11" x 11"

70

71

72

73

74

75
Artist: **JAMES McMULLAN**
Art Director: Suzanne Morin
Client: Audubon Magazine
Medium: Watercolor, gouache on paper
Size: 5" x 8"

76
Artist: **GUY BILLOUT**
Art Director: Judy Garlan
Client: The Atlantic Monthly
Medium: Watercolor, airbrush on
      Bristol vellum
Size: 10" x 7"

77
Artist: **STEVEN GUARNACCIA**
Art Director: Italo Lupi
Client: Abitare
Medium: Watercolor
Size: 13" x 10"

78
Artist: **STEVEN GUARNACCIA**
Art Director: Italo Lupi
Client: Abitare
Medium: Watercolor
Size: 13" x 10"

79
Artist: **KINUKO Y. CRAFT**
Art Director: Tom Staebler
Client: Playboy
Medium: Gouache on paper
Size: 15" x 15"

75

76

EDITORIAL

77

78

79

80
Artist: **ISTVAN BANYAI**
Art Director: Tom Staebler
Client: Playboy

81
Artist: **GUY BILLOUT**
Art Director: Judy Garlan
Client: The Atlantic Monthly
Medium: Watercolor, airbrush on
Bristol vellum
Size: 9" x 7"

82
Artist: **VICKY RABINOWICZ**
Art Director: Linda Birch
Client: Electronic Musician
Medium: Linoleum cut collage,
mixed media on paper
Size: 14" x 10"

83
Artist: **BRAD HOLLAND**
Art Director: Nancy Canfield
Client: Chicago Tribune Magazine
Medium: Acrylic on masonite
Size: 15" x 12"

84
Artist: **VICKY RABINOWICZ**
Art Director: Richard Boddy
Client: Discover
Medium: Linoleum cut collage on paper
Size: 8" x 7"

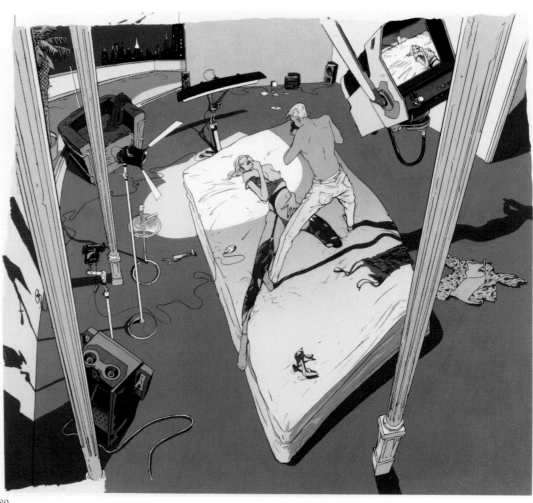

80

81

82

83

84

85
Artist: **BRUCE McCALL**
Art Director: David Harris
Client: Vanity Fair
Medium: Gouache
Size: 13" x 10"

86
Artist: **JOE CIARDIELLO**
Art Director: Howard Brown
Client: Urban Outfitters
Medium: Pen & ink on paper
Size: 10" x 8"

87
Artist: **HANOCH PIVEN**
Art Directors: Syndi Becker
Marcos Villaca
Client: New York
Medium: Collage on paper
Size: 13" x 11"

88
Artist: **HANOCH PIVEN**
Art Directors: Dov Alfon
Maya Wallach
Client: Haaretz
Medium: Collage on paper
Size: 16" x 15"

89
Artist: **HANOCH PIVEN**
Art Directors: Dov Alfon
Maya Wallach
Client: Haaretz
Medium: Collage on paper
Size: 13" x 9"

90
Artist: **ALAN E. COBER**
Art Director: Andy Kner
Client: Scenario
Medium: Dry point, watercolor on
Arches cover
Size: 10" x 9"

91
Artist: **ALAN E. COBER**
Art Director: David Matt
Client: Premier Magazine
Medium: Ink, watercolor on
140 Arches cold press
Size: 10" x 6"

85

86

87

88

89

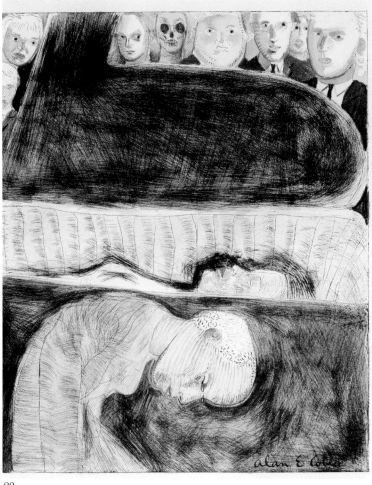

90

91

92
Artist: **WILSON McLEAN**
Art Director: Tom Staebler
Client: Playboy
Medium: Oil on canvas
Size: 23" x 19"

93
Artist: **ROB DAY**
Art Director: Robert Priest
Client: Gentlemen's Quarterly
Medium: Oil on paper
Size: 8" x 8"

94
Artist: **ROB DAY**
Art Director: David Matt
Client: Premiere Magazine
Medium: Oil on paper
Size: 14" x 11"

95
Artist: **CHRISTIAN CLAYTON**
Art Directors: Fred Woodward
Gail Anderson
Client: Rolling Stone
Medium: Acrylic on paper
Size: 13" x 9"

96
Artist: **ANDREA VENTURA**
Art Director: Chris Curry
Client: The New Yorker
Medium: Acrylic on paper
Size: 18" x 20"

92

93

94

95

96

97
Artist: **PETER DE SÈVE**
Art Director: Françoise Mouly
Client: The New Yorker
Medium: Watercolor
Size: 15" x 10"

98
Artist: **CHRISTIAN NORTHEAST**
Art Director: Deanna Lowe
Client: New York
Size: 10" x 8"

99
Artist: **PETER DE SÈVE**
Art Director: Françoise Mouly
Client: The New Yorker
Medium: Watercolor
Size: 16" x 11"

100
Artist: **RICK SEALOCK**
Art Director: D. J. Stout
Client: Texas Monthly
Medium: Mixed on watercolor paper
Size: 13" x 9"

97

98

99

100

101
Artist: **JANET WOOLLEY**
Art Director: Gail Anderson
Client: Rolling Stone
Medium: Mixed
Size: 15" x 18"

102
Artist: **ANDREA VENTURA**
Art Director: Fred Woodward
Client: Rolling Stone
Size: 13" x 8"

103
Artist: **ANDREA VENTURA**
Art Director: Steven Heller
Client: The New York Times
Book Review
Medium: Acrylic
Size: 14" x 13"

104
Artist: **GARY KELLEY**
Art Directors: Chris Curry
Nick Parker
Client: The New Yorker
Medium: Pastel over Monotype
Size: 18" x 12"

105
Artist: **MARCO VENTURA**
Art Director: Kenneth B. Smith
Client: Time
Medium: Oil on paper
Size: 9" x 7"

101

102

103

104

105

106
Artist: **DANIEL ADEL**
Art Director: Amy Rosenfeld
Client: Smart Money
Medium: Oil on board
Size: 10" x 8"

107
Artist: **DANIEL ADEL**
Art Director: Deanna Lowe
Client: New York
Size: 10" x 8"

108
Artist: **DANIEL ADEL**
Art Director: Pam Zelenz
Client: Golf Magazine
Medium: Oil on panel
Size: 10" x 8"

109
Artist: **JULIAN ALLEN**
Art Director: Steven Heller
Client: The New York Times
Medium: Oil on paper
Size: 12" x 14"

106

107

108

109

110
Artist: **JOHN COLLIER**
Art Director: Amy Osborn
Client: Los Angeles Magazine
Medium: Watercolor, pastel
Size: 24" x 15"

111
Artist: **PAUL DAVIS**
Art Director: Fred Woodward
Client: Rolling Stone
Medium: Acrylic on board
Size: 18" x 24"

112
Artist: **MILTON GLASER**
Art Director: Fred Woodward
Client: Rolling Stone
Medium: Colored pencil on paper

113
Artist: **PIERRE LE-TAN**
Art Director: Chris Curry
Client: The New Yorker
Medium: Pen & ink, watercolor

110

111

112

113

B O O K   J U R Y

VINCENT DiFATE, Chair
Illustrator

MICHAEL J. DEAS
Illustrator

PETER FIORE
Illustrator

SUSAN JEFFERS
Illustrator

STEPHEN T. JOHNSON
Illustrator

STEVEN STROUD
Illustrator

MARK SUMMERS
Illustrator

DAVID WILCOX
Illustrator

SCOTT YARDLEY
Art Director
Good Housekeeping

BOOK

••••••••••••••••••••••••••••••••

Award
Winners

••••••••••••••••••••••••

CARTER GOODRICH
Gold Medal

GENNEDY SPIRIN
Gold Medal

MARK BUEHNER
Silver Medal

KINUKO Y. CRAFT
Silver Medal

TIM RAGLIN
Silver Medal

114
Artist: **CARTER GOODRICH**

Art Director: Barbara Fitzsimmons

Client: William Morrow Junior Books

Medium: Colored pencil, watercolor
on board

Size: 12" x 16"

Book Gold Medal
CARTER GOODRICH

"It had been my hope that this piece would double as the jacket art for *A Christmas Carol.* Unfortunately, that didn't turn out to be the case. Like all the other illustrations in the book, this one had a difficult birth. That, and the nagging concern as to whether or not this story should be done again at all, kept a shadow of uncertainty over the project for me. This totally unexpected honor coming from the Society has done an awful lot to help lift that doubt."

115

Artist: **GENNEDY SPIRIN**

Art Director: Amelia Lau Carling

Client: Dial Books for Young Readers

Medium: Watercolor, pencil

Size: 10" x 18"

Book Gold Medal
GENNEDY SPIRIN
This is Gennedy Spirin's fourth Gold medal in the past five years for a work published by Dial Books for Young Readers. The surreal humanity he adds to his consummate artistic training, which he received in Moscow, has led to his many awards. This scene from *The Tsar of Saltan* depicts the sad moment when the Tsarina and her child are cast adrift in a barrel by order of the Tsar.

116
Artist: **MARK BUEHNER**
Art Director: Nancy Leo
Client: Dial Books for Young Readers
Medium: Oil over acrylic on masonite
Size: 14" x 18"

Book Silver Medal
MARK BUEHNER
"This illustration is taken from the book *Fanny's Dream*, written by my wife, Caralyn. The story is loosely based on the lives of Cara's grandparents who worked, married, and raised a family on a farm in Lovell, Wyoming. The farm is now being worked by Cara's aunt and uncle, so we packed up our family and drove to Lovell where I took pictures and got a feeling for the lay of the land. I wanted to portray Fanny and Heber as being solid, salt-of-the-earth people. This scene depicts Fanny thinking over Heber's marriage proposal. I wanted to show the common human awkwardness that we often feel at times like these."

117
Artist: **KINUKO Y. CRAFT**
Art Director: Barbara Fitzsimmons
Client: William Morrow Junior Books
Medium: Watercolor, oil on board
Size: 15" x 12"

Book Silver Medal
KINUKO Y. CRAFT
Here, Cupid, the God of Love, and Psyche, the personification of the human soul, play out their tortured affair to the bemusements of the Gods. Kinuko Y. Craft's complicated compositions throughout the book made it difficult to reach her deadline. But her style allows no cut corners and no shortcuts. Perhaps the image of Psyche depicted here, reflects Kinuko after the messenger left her Connecticut studio with the finished book in hand.

118
Artist: **TIM RAGLIN**

Art Director: Gerald McConnell

Client: Madison Square Press

Medium: Pen & Ink

Size: 13" x 23"

Book Silver Medal

TIM RAGLIN

"This scene from *Uncle Mugsy* is one I have been "rehearsing" since, as a child, I was first interested in picture books and drawing. That the process has led to the Society of Illustrators Silver Medal is therefore deeply gratifying to me. Thank you."

119
Artist: **DAVID BOWERS**
Art Director: Julia Kushnirsky
Client: St. Martin's Press
Medium: Oil on masonite
Size: 17" x 10"

120
Artist: **MARY GRANDPRÉ**
Art Director: Gail Dubov
Client: Avon Books
Medium: Pastel
Size: 16" x 14"

121
Artist: **DENNIS NOLAN**
Art Director: Atha Tehon
Client: Dial Books for Young Readers
Medium: Watercolor, graphite on paper
Size: 15" x 12"

119

120

121

122
Artist: **MIKE REED**
Art Director: Celia Chetham
Client: Houghton Mifflin
Medium: Acrylic on board
Size: 17" x 20"

123
Artist: **CHARLES SANTORE**
Art Director: Don Bender
Client: Random House Value
Publishing, Inc.
Medium: Watercolor on Arches
Size: 13" x 20"

124
Artist: **JOHN THOMPSON**
Art Director: Elizabeth B. Parisi
Client: Scholastic
Medium: Acrylic on board
Size: 18" x 12"

125
Artist: **DAVE KRAMER**
Medium: Oil on board
Size: 23" x 15"

122

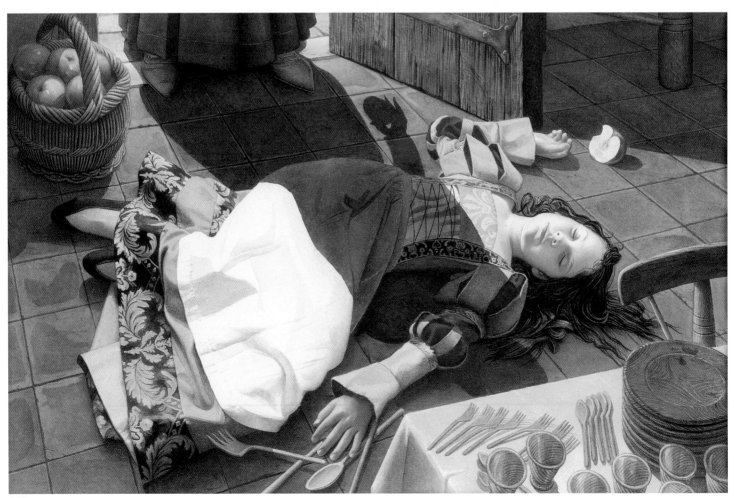

123

124

125

126
Artist: **SEAN P. LYNCH**
Medium: Oil with Liquin on wood panel
Size: 15" x 17"

127
Artist: **WILLIAM C. ERSLAND**
Art Director: Lynne Bertalmio
Client: Floating Fish Quarterly Review
Medium: Acrylic on canvas
Size: 18" x 14"

128
Artist: **HERBERT TAUSS**
Art Directors: Ellen Dreyer
　　　　　　Barbara Fitzsimmons
Client: William Morrow Junior Books
Medium: Charcoal on canvas
Size: 16" x 26"

129
Artist: **EDWARD ABRAMS**
Art Directors: B. Martin Pedersen
　　　　　　Randell Pearson
Client: Graphis
Medium: Etching on Fabriano
　　　　Murillo cream
Size: 5" x 5"

126

127

128

129

130
Artist: **BERNIE FUCHS**
Art Director: Sheila Smallwood
Client: Little Brown
Medium: Oil on canvas
Size: 28" x 19"

131
Artist: **JOHN JUDE PALENCAR**
Art Director: Anne Twomey
Client: St. Martin's Press
Size: 14" x 26"

132
Artist: **DENNIS LYALL**
Art Director: Matt Galemmos
Client: Pocket Books
Medium: Oil on board
Size: 14" x 23"

130

131

132

132 Detail

133
Artist: **BRAD SNEED**
Art Director: Nancy Leo
Client: Dial Books for Young Readers
Medium: Oil on gessoed cold press
watercolor paper
Size: 13" x 13"

134
Artist: **SERGEI GOLOSHAPOV**
Art Director: Sergei Goloshapov
Client: North-South Books, Inc.
Medium: Watercolor, ink, pastel on paper
Size: 16" x 9"

135
Artist: **SERGEI GOLOSHAPOV**
Art Director: Sergei Goloshapov
Client: North-South Books, Inc.
Medium: Watercolor, ink, pastel on paper
Size: 14" x 9"

136
Artist: **MICHAEL WHELAN**
Art Director: Arnie Fenner
Client: Ziesing Publications
Medium: Oil on Arches watercolor board
Size: 22" x 22"

133

134

135

136

137
Artist: **MURRAY TINKELMAN**
Art Director: Judi Smalling
Client: Beckett Publishing
Medium: Pen & ink on Bristol
(Plate Finish)
Size: 18" x 13"

138
Artist: **HERBERT TAUSS**
Art Directors: Ellen Dreyer
Barbara Fitzsimmons
Client: William Morrow Junior Books
Medium: Charcoal on canvas
Size: 19" x 14"

139
Artist: **MARK ULRIKSEN**
Art Director: Chris Curry
Client: The New Yorker
Size: 7" x 7"

140
Artist: **MARK ULRIKSEN**
Art Director: Philip Bratter
Client: Worth
Medium: Acrylic on paper
Size: 16" x 23"

137

138

139

140

141
Artist: **HAYDN CORNNER**
Art Director: Tom Egner
Client: Avon Books
Medium: Oil on board
Size: 18" x 12"

142
Artist: **JAMES BENNETT**
Art Director: Gail Dubov
Client: Avon Books
Medium: Oil on board
Size: 12" x 9"

143
Artist: **JACK ENDEWELT**
Medium: Oil on Strathmore board
Size: 9" x 12"

144
Artist: **JOE CEPEDA**
Art Directors: Lucille Chomowicz
Anahid Hamparian
Client: Simon & Schuster
Medium: Oil, montage on board

141

142

143

144

145

Artist: **TIM O'BRIEN**

Art Director: Elizbeth B. Parisi

Client: Scholastic

Medium: Oil on gessoed panel

Size: 14" x 10"

146

Artist: **JOHN JUDE PALENCAR**

Art Director: Don Puckey

Client: Warner Books

Medium: Acrylic on Strathmore

Size: 12" x 13"

147

Artist: **GREG COUCH**

Art Directors: Lucille Chomowicz
Paul Zakris

Client: Simon & Schuster

Medium: Colored pencil, acrylic on
museum board

Size: 12" x 19"

148

Artist: **VICTOR STABIN**

Art Director: Judith Murello

Client: Berkley Publishing Group

Size: 18" x 24"

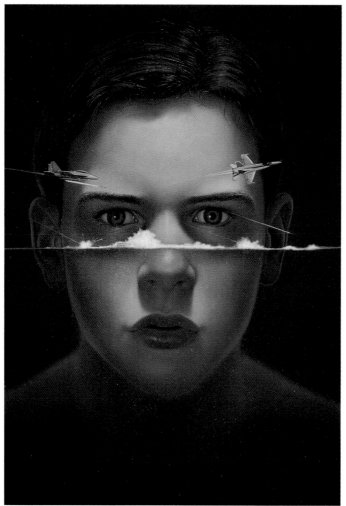

145

146

147

148

149
Artist: **MARK SUMMERS**

Art Director: Elizabeth B. Parisi

Client: Scholastic

Medium: Scratchboard

Size: 7" x 7"

150
Artist: **DONATO GIANCOLA**

Art Director: David Stevenson

Client: Ballantine Books

Medium: Oil, painted on primed
Arches 90lb drawing
paper mounted on Masonite

Size: 26" x 18"

151
Artist: **KAZUHIKO SANO**

Art Directors: Sachiko Sakurai
Shuichi Ogata

Client: Shinchosha

Medium: Acrylic on Masonite

Size: 20" x 15"

152
Artist: **BILL NELSON**

Medium: 3-Dimensional sculpture
mixed media

Size: 16" x 8"

149

150

151

152

153
Artist: **CRAIG TENNANT**
Client: Cheryl Anderson
Medium: Oil on canvas

154
Artist: **STEPHEN T. JOHNSON**
Art Director: Sara Reynolds
Client: Dutton Books
Medium: Pastel, watercolor on
Arches hot press paper
Size: 20" x 13"

155
Artist: **CRAIG TENNANT**
Client: Cheyenne Press
Medium: Oil on canvas

156
Artist: **CRAIG TENNANT**
Medium: Oil on canvas

153

154

155

156

157
Artist: **WILSON McLEAN**
Client: RotoVision SA
Medium: Oil on canvas
Size: 29" x 23"

158
Artist: **KENT WILLIAMS**
Art Director: Richard Thomas
Client: White Wolf Inc.
Medium: Mixed on paper mounted on
        wood panel
Size: 23" x 18"

159
Artist: **KENT WILLIAMS**
Art Director: Robbin Brosterman
Client: DC/Vertigo Comics
Medium: Mixed on paper mounted on
        wood panel
Size: 26" x 17"

160
Artist: **JOEL SPECTOR**
Art Director: Ann Huizenga
Client: Zondervan Corp.
Medium: Pastel
Size: 28" x 28"

157

158

159

160

161
Artist: **DANIEL CRAIG**
Art Director: Paul Buckley
Client: Penguin USA
Medium: Acrylic on ragboard
Size: 22" x 15"

162
Artist: **MARK HESS**
Art Director: Carl Galian
Client: Penguin USA
Medium: Acrylic on canvas
Size: 10" x 10"

163
Artist: **ROBERT GOLDSTROM**
Art Director: Diane Luger
Client: Warner Books
Medium: Oil on canvas
Size: 13" x 9"

161

162

163

164
Artist: **M. PARASKEVAS**
Art Director: Michael Farmer
Client: Harcourt Brace
Medium: Acrylic on Srathmore board

165
Artist: **DANIEL KIRK**
Art Director: Julia Gorton
Client: Hyperion Press
Medium: Oil on canvas
Size: 15" x 16"

166
Artist: **WENDELL MINOR**
Art Director: Michael Lindgren
Client: Zoland Books, Inc.
Medium: Watercolor on cold press paper
Size: 4" x 8"

167
Artist: **BRUCE WALDMAN**
Art Director: Lauron Dong
Client: Crown Publishers
Medium: Monoprint on paper
Size: 29" x 21"

164

165

166

167

168
Artist: **BRAD HOLLAND**
Art Director: D. K. Holland
Client: Rockport Allworth
Medium: Pastel on handmade paper
Size: 12" x 9"

169
Artist: **JOHN JUDE PALENCAR**
Art Director: David Stevenson
Client: Random House
Medium: Acrylic on Strathmore
Size: 13" x 38"

170
Artist: **DAVID SHANNON**
Art Director: Lisa Peters
Client: Harcourt Brace
Medium: Acrylic on board
Size: 14" x 12"

171
Artist: **NICHOLAS WILTON**
Art Director: Lucille Chomowicz
Client: Simon & Schuster
Medium: Acrylic on pine wood
Size: 8" x 6"

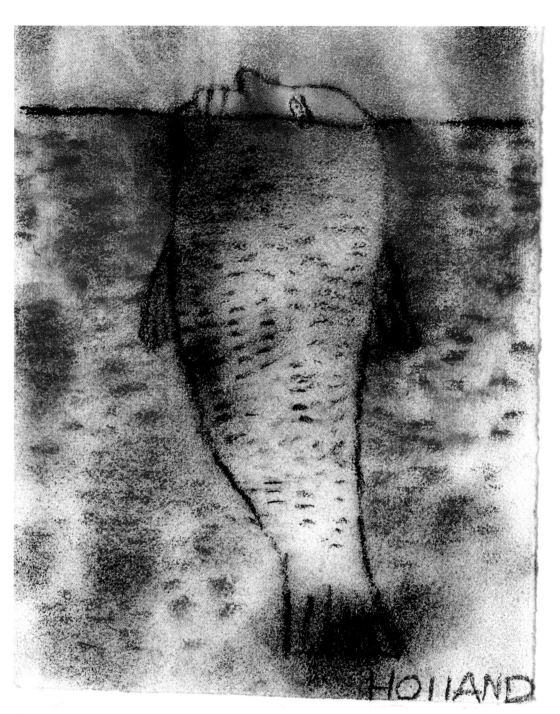

168

169

170

171

172
Artist: **CATHLEEN TOELKE**
Art Director: Jack Seow
Client: Simon & Schuster
Medium: Gouache on watercolor board
Size: 12" x 8"

173
Artist: **GLENN HARRINGTON**
Art Director: Susan Lu Bassard
Medium: Oil on board
Size: 19" x 13"

174
Artist: **MITCHELL HOOKS**
Art Director: Barbara Leff
Client: Random House-Fawcett Books
Medium: Oil
Size: 23" x 14"

175
Artist: **MITCHELL HOOKS**
Art Director: Barbara Leff
Client: Random House-Fawcett Books
Medium: Oil
Size: 23" x 14"

172

173

174

175

176
Artist: **KINUKO Y. CRAFT**
Art Director: Barbara Fitzsimmons
Client: William Morrow Junior Books
Medium: Watercolor, oil on board
Size: 15" x 12"

177
Artist: **KINUKO Y. CRAFT**
Art Director: Barbara Fitzsimmons
Client: William Morrow Junior Books
Medium: Watercolor, oil on board
Size: 15" x 12"

178
Artist: **LEO & DIANE DILLON**
Art Director: Nicholas Krenitsky
Client: HarperCollins
Medium: Pastel, acrylic on Strathmore
Bristol board
Size: 16" x 11"

179
Artist: **DAVID GROVE**
Art Director: Angelo Perrone
Client: Reader's Digest Condensed
Books
Medium: Gouache, acrylic on gessoed
board
Size: 16" x 11"

176

177

178

179

180

Artist: **CARTER GOODRICH**

Art Director: Barbara Fitzsimmons

Client: William Morrow Junior Books

Medium: Colored pencil, watercolor on board

Size: 17" x 12"

181

Artist: **CARTER GOODRICH**

Art Director: Barbara Fitzsimmons

Client: William Morrow Junior Books

Medium: Colored pencil, watercolor on board

Size: 16" x 12"

182

Artist: **CARTER GOODRICH**

Art Director: Barbara Fitzsimmons

Client: William Morrow Junior Books

Medium: Colored pencil, watercolor on board

Size: 17" x 12"

183

Artist: **BLAIR DRAWSON**

Client: Orchard Books

Medium: Acrylic

Size: 11" x 20"

180

181

182

183

184
Artist: **ROBERT GOLDSTROM**
Art Director: John Fontana
Client: Scribner's
Medium: Oil on canvas
Size: 13" x 9"

185
Artist: **WENDELL MINOR**
Art Director: Al Cetta
Client: HarperCollins
Medium: Acrylic on masonite
Size: 10" x 12"

186
Artist: **BILL NELSON**
Art Director: Robert Fillie
Client: Billboard Books
Medium: Colored pencil on Strathmore paper
Size: 14" x 9"

187
Artist: **TIM O'BRIEN**
Art Director: Elizbeth B. Parisi
Client: Scholastic
Medium: Oil on board
Size: 17" x 11"

188
Artist: **DONATO GIANCOLA**
Art Director: David Stevenson
Client: Ballantine Books
Medium: Oil, painted on primed Arches 90lb drawing paper mounted on Masonite
Size: 21" x 33"

184

185

186

187

188

189

Artist: **EDWARD GAZSI**

Art Director: Christine Kettner

Client: HarperCollins

Medium: Acrylic on masonite

Size: 9" x 6"

190

Artist: **JERRY PINKNEY**

Art Director: Atha Tehon

Client: Dial Books for Young Readers

Medium: Watercolor

Size: 10" x 21"

191

Artist: **BILL MAYER**

Art Director: Mary Ellen Podgorski

Client: Klutz Press

Medium: Dyes, gouache

Size: 9" x 13"

192

Artist: **GREGORY MANCHESS**

Art Director: B. Martin Pedersen

Client: Graphis

Medium: Oil on gessoed board

Size: 11" x 6"

189

190

191

193
Artist: **EDWARD GAZSI**
Art Director: Christine Kettner
Client: HarperCollins
Medium: Acrylic on masonite
Size: 9" x 6"

194
Artist: **LOREN LONG**
Art Director: Loren Long
Client: Bear Graphics and Illustration
  Gallery
Medium: Acrylic on board
Size: 14" x 10"

195
Artist: **PETER DE SÈVE**
Art Director: Amy King
Client: Doubleday Books
Medium: Watercolor
Size: 19" x 15"

196
Artist: **VINCENT DiFATE**
Art Director: Sheila Gilbert
Client: DAW Books, Inc.
Medium: Acrylics on gessoed hardboard
Size: 16" x 24"

193

194

195

197
Artist: **TRISTAN A. ELWELL**
Art Director: Irene Gallo
Client: TOR Books
Medium: Oil, acrylic on masonite
Size: 23" x 17"

198
Artist: **JOANIE SCHWARZ**
Art Director: Isabel Warren Lynch
Client: Alfred A. Knopf
Medium: Digital, dye
Size: 10" x 9"

199
Artist: **GENNEDY SPIRIN**
Art Director: Gennady Spirin
Client: The Putnam & Grosset Group
Medium: Watercolor
Size: 20" x 17"

200
Artist: **DAVID SHANNON**
Art Director: Kathleen Westray
Client: Scholastic
Medium: Acrylic on board

197

198

199

201

Artist: **TROY HOWELL**

Art Directors: Cecilia Yung
Donna Mark

Client: The Putnam & Grosset Group

Medium: Acrylic

Size: 9" x 14"

202

Artist: **LAURA SEELEY**

Art Director: Loraine Balcsik

Client: Peachtree Publishers, Ltd.

Medium: Mixed on cold press board

Size: 11" x 6"

203

Artist: **CHARLES SANTORE**

Art Director: Don Bender

Client: Random House Value
Publishing, Inc.

Medium: Watercolor on Arches

Size: 13" x 20"

204

Artist: **HONI WERNER**

Art Director: Jim Plumeri

Client: Bantam Books

Medium: Digital illustration,
dye sublimation print

Size: 9" x 7"

201

202

203

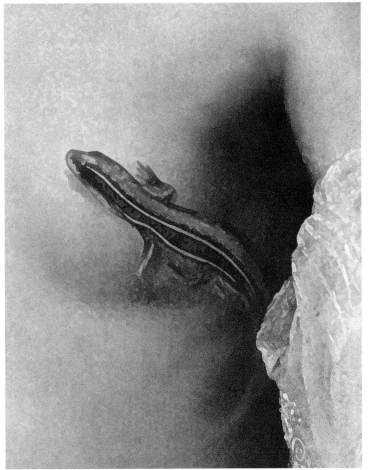

204

205
Artist: **WENDELL MINOR**
Art Director: Anne Diebel
Client: Clarion Books
Medium: Acrylic on masonite panel
Size: 12" x 20"

206
Artist: **WILLIAM LOW**
Art Director: Mary Schuck
Client: Simon & Schuster
Medium: Oil
Size: 27" x 14"

207
Artist: **TIM O'BRIEN**
Art Director: Elizbeth B. Parisi
Client: Scholastic
Medium: Oil on board
Size: 14" x 9"

208
Artist: **JOHN CLAPP**
Art Directors: Lucille Chomowicz
Paul Zakris
Client: Simon & Schuster Books for
Young Readers
Medium: Watercolor on paper
Size: 10" x 6"

209
Artist: **STEPHEN T. JOHNSON**
Art Director: Irene Gallo
Client: Tor Books
Medium: Pastel, watercolor on Arches
hot press paper
Size: 23" x 16"

205

206

207

208

209

210
Artist: **GARY KELLEY**
Art Director: Rita Marshall
Client: Creative Editions
Medium: Pastel over Monotype
Size: 14" x 22"

211
Artist: **GARY KELLEY**
Art Director: Rita Marshall
Client: Creative Editions
Medium: Pastel over Monotype
Size: 18" x 12"

212
Artist: **WILLIAM JOYCE**
Art Director: Christine Kettner
Client: HarperCollins
Medium: Oil on Bristol board
Size: 21" x 21"

213
Artist: **WILLIAM JOYCE**
Art Director: Christine Kettner
Client: HarperCollins
Medium: Oil on Bristol board

210

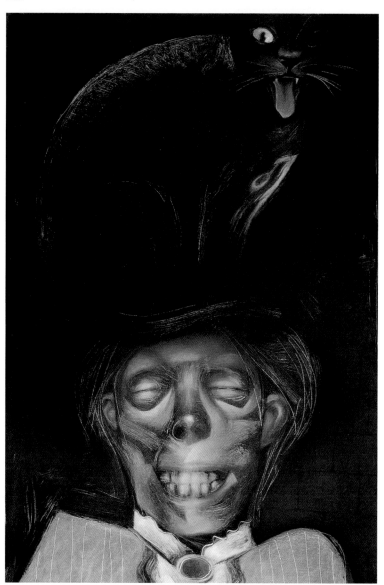

211

212

214
Artist: **DAVID BOWERS**
Art Director: Jerry Todd
Client: St. Martin's Press
Medium: Oil on masonite
Size: 19" x 12"

215
Artist: **JAMES DIETZ**
Art Director: Fred Jungclaus
Client: Indianapolis Motor Speedway
Museum
Medium: Oil on canvas

216
Artist: **JOHN H. HOWARD**
Art Director: George Cornell
Client: Penguin USA
Medium: Acrylic on canvas
Size: 35" x 23"

217
Artist: **TED COCONIS**
Art Director: Soren Noring
Client: Reader's Digest Condensed
Books
Medium: Oil, acrylic on board
Size: 26" x 21"

214

215

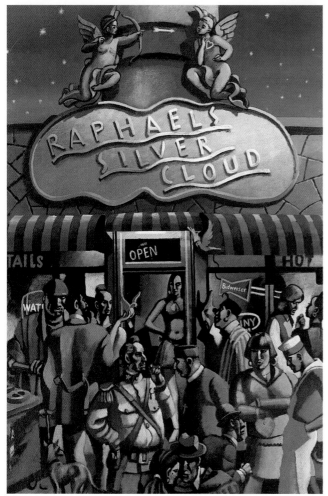

216

217

218
Artist: **KINUKO Y. CRAFT**
Art Director: Diane Luger
Client: Warner Books
Medium: Oil on board
Size: 23" x 24"

219
Artist: **PETER FIORE**
Art Director: Becky Loughlin
Client: Viking Penguin
Medium: Oil
Size: 14" x 11"

220
Artist: **PETER FIORE**
Art Director: Leslie Bauman
Client: Troll Communications Museum
Medium: Oil on board
Size: 15" x 12"

221
Artist: **PETER FIORE**
Art Director: Paolo Pepe
Client: Washington Square Press
Medium: Oil
Size: 26" x17"

222
Artist: **GREG HARLIN**
Art Director: Elizabeth B. Parisi
Client: Scholastic
Medium: Watercolor on
　　　Strathmore board
Size: 10" x 21"

218

219

220

221

222

223

Artist: **WAYNE BARLOWE**

Art Director: James Cowan

Medium: Acrylic on rag board

Size: 17" x 26"

224

Artist: **JEFF CROSBY**

Medium: Intaglio, Aquatint on paper

Size: 13" x 6"

225

Artist: **DON DAILY**

Art Director: Paul Kepple

Client: Running Press

Medium: Watercolor on Arches
watercolor paper

Size: 13" x 9"

226

Artist: **ANDREW DAVIDSON**

Art Director: Amy Hill

Client: Simon & Schuster

Medium: Woodcut engraving

Size: 6" x 5"

227

Artist: **ANDREW DAVIDSON**

Art Director: Amy Hill

Client: Simon & Schuster

Medium: Woodcut engraving

Size: 6" x 5"

223

224

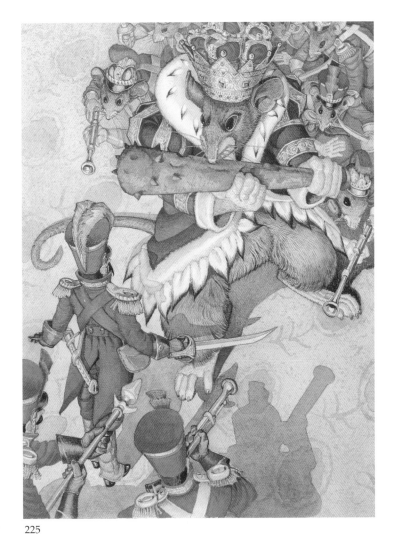

225

226

227

228
Artist: **MARK ENGLISH**
Art Director: Jim Plumeri
Client: Bantam Books

229
Artist: **RAÚL COLÓN**
Art Director: Stefanie Rosenfeld
Client: Penguin USA/Puffin Books
Medium: Pencil, watercolor on Fabriano
    watercolor paper
Size: 13" x 8"

230
Artist: **RAÚL COLÓN**
Art Director: Nick Krenitsky
Client: HarperCollins
Medium: Acrylic
Size: 15" x 10"

231
Artist: **GREG HARLIN**
Art Director: Angelo Perrone
Client: Reader's Digest
Medium: Watercolor on
    Strathmore board
Size: 12" x 17"

228

229

230

231

ADVERTISING JURY

BARBARA NESSIM, Chair
*Illustrator/Parsons School of
Design, Illustration Department*

RICHARD BERENSON
*Worldwide Art Director
Reader's Digest*

DAVID BOWERS
Illustrator

ALAN E. COBER
Artist, educator

MICHAEL GARLAND
Illustrator

CARL HERRMAN
*Art Director
U.S. Postal Service*

JAMES McMULLAN
Illustrator, poster designer

GREG SPALENKA
Illustrator

ADVERTISING

· ·

Award
Winners

· · · · · · · · · · · · · · · ·

JOE SORREN
Gold Medal

MICHAEL WHELAN
Gold Medal

CHRISTIAN CLAYTON
Silver Medal

C.F. PAYNE
Silver Medal

232
Artist: **JOE SORREN**
Art Directors: Joe Sorren
Stephen Motley
Client: Sparklepoop International
Medium: Acrylic on canvas
Size: 35" x 35"

Adverstising Gold Medal
JOE SORREN
"I'm not too sure what to say about this painting except that it was modeled after my daughter Martha and her first experience with makeup. I think it is as much her medal as mine, if not more."

233
Artist: **MICHAEL WHELAN**

Art Director: Monte Conner

Client: Roadrunner Records

Medium: Digital collage,
Photoshop 2.5, PowerMac

Size: 16" x 16"

Adverstising Gold Medal
MICHAEL WHELAN
Whelan has been interested in science fiction and fantasy imagery since his early childhood. In the past 21 years he has created hundreds of paintings for book covers, calendars, magazines, and record albums for which he has garnered virtually all awards in the international fields of fantasy and science fiction art. He has won three "Howard" awards and 13 "Hugos," as well as a "SuperHugo"for Best Professional Artist of the last 50 years. *Locus* magazine readers have named him "Best Artist" for 17 years running. His work is "at its most fundamental level, about creating a 'sense of wonder.' "

234
Artist: **CHRISTIAN CLAYTON**

Art Director: Rick Patrick

Client: Mercury Records

Medium: Acrylic, pencil, pen & ink on cut paper

Size: 12" x 12"

Adverstising Silver Medal
CHRISTIAN CLAYTON
A graduate of the Art Center College of Design, Christian Clayton's work has been recognized by *American Illustration, Communication Arts, Print* and the Society of Illustrators. He lives and works in Los Angeles where he teaches at the Art Center.

235
Artist: **C. F. PAYNE**

Art Director: Joe Pompeo

Agency: Saatchi & Saatchi

Client: Florida Citrus Growers

Medium: Oil, acrylic, watercolor, colored pencil on board

Size: 16" x 13"

Adverstising Silver Medal
C.F. PAYNE

"The illustration world gives me the chance to grow as an artist through the work I get—it makes the hard work a pleasure."

236
Artist: **DANIEL ADEL**
Art Director: Tom Tagariello
Client: Time
Medium: Oil on panel
Size: 15" x 20"

237
Artist: **RAFAL OLBINSKI**
Art Director: Jane Ohye
Agency: Nappi Eliran Murphy
Client: New York City Opera
Medium: Acrylic on canvas

238
Artist: **KINUKO Y. CRAFT**
Art Directors: Kathleen Ryan
Collene Currie
Client: Dallas Opera
Medium: Watercolor, oil on paper
Size: 28" x 24"

239
Artist: **DAVID BOWERS**
Art Director: David Whitmore
Client: TLC Monthly /
The Learning Channel
Medium: Oil, crackling varnish on
gessoed masonite
Size: 16" x 11"

240
Artist: **DAVID BOWERS**
Art Director: Michele Perfetto
Agency: Hill Holliday
Client: Latrobe Brewing
Medium: Oil on masonite
Size: 13" x 33"

236

237

238

239

240

241

Artist: **WARREN LINN**

Art Director: Mark Ulrich

Client: Workbook

Medium: Mixed on masonite

Size: 24" x 19"

242

Artist: **BILL MAYER**

Art Director: Andrea Hemman

Client: Seven Arts

Medium: Dyes, gouache

243

Artist: **COCO MASUDA**

Art Director: Ellen Weinberger

Agency: Ingalls, Quinn & Johnson

Client: Ingalls, Quinn & Johnson

Medium: Airbrush, acrylic, colored pencil on paper

Size: 15" x 10"

244

Artist: **WARREN LINN**

Art Directors: Barbara Nessim
Robin Malik

Client: Musician Magazine/
Parsons School of Design

Medium: Mixed on wood

Size: 24" x 15"

241

242

243

244

245
Artist: **DAVID E. LESH**
Art Director: Arthur Anderson
Client: Arthur Anderson Consulting
Medium: Mixed
Size: 12" x 9"

246
Artist: **AMY GUIP**
Art Directors: Tommy Steele
George Mimnaugh
Client: Capitol Records

247
Artist: **DAVID E. LESH**
Medium: Mixed
Size: 8" x 9"

248
Artist: **STEPHANIE GARCIA**
Art Director: Margery Greenspan
Client: Polygram Records
Medium: Mixed on wood and metal
Size: 14" x 14"

245

246

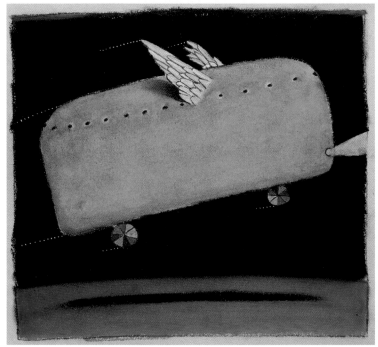

247

248

249
Artist: **PETER DE SÈVE**
Art Director: Sandy Block
Client: Serino Coyne Inc.
Medium: Watercolor on paper
Size: 16" x 9"

250
Artist: **JACK UNRUH**
Art Director: Karen Holland
Agency: Ogilvy & Mather
Client: Child Advocates
Medium: Ink, watercolor on board
Size: 13" x 18"

251
Artist: **JACK UNRUH**
Art Director: Tim Parker
Agency: Sasquach
Client: Leatherman
Medium: Ink, watercolor on board
Size: 19" x 16"

249

252
Artist: **COLBERT GAUTHIER**

Art Directors: Nick Cusick
              Laura Schwisow

Client: Bison Recreational Products

Medium: Oil on gessoed board

Size: 25" x 19"

253
Artist: **RAFAL OLBINSKI**

Art Director: Rafal Olbinski

Client: New York City Opera

Medium: Acrylic on canvas

254
Artist: **BRAD HOLLAND**

Art Director: Erwin Piplits

Client: Odeon Theatre

Medium: Acrylic on masonite

Size: 26" x 19"

255
Artist: **BRAD HOLLAND**

Art Director: Bernard Schmidtobreick

Client: Deutscher Caritasverband

Medium: Acrylic on masonite

Size: 17" x 14"

252

253

254

255

256
Artist: **ALBERT LORENZ**
Art Director: Darilyn Lowe Carnes
Client: Harry N. Abrams, Inc.
Medium: Mixed on 2-ply Bristol
Size: 19" x 28"

257
Artist: **ALBERT LORENZ**
Art Director: Richard Dezzino
Client: Bepuzzled
Medium: Mixed on 2-ply Bristol
Size: 30" x 40"

258
Artist: **EUGENE HOFFMAN**
Art Director: Eugene Hoffman
Client: The Pressworks Denver
Medium: Cardboard 3-D

259
Artist: **JOHN H. HOWARD**
Art Directors: Sheryl Yasger
　　　　　　　Nancy Owens
Client: Dean Whitter Reynolds Inc.
Medium: Acrylic on canvas
Size: 36" x 48"

256

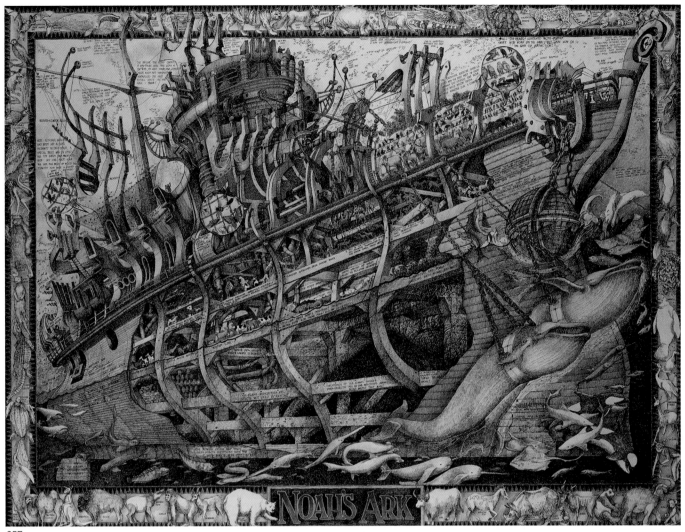

257

257

259

260
Artist: **THOMAS L. FLUHARTY**

Art Director: David Stevenson

Agency: McCann Erickson

Client: Coca-Cola

Medium: Acrylic on Bristol

Size: 17" x 13"

261
Artist: **MITCH GREENBLATT**

Art Director: Darren Johnson

Client: Warner Bros. Records

Medium: Mixed on wood, clay

Size: 23" x 23"

262
Artist: **GREGORY MANCHESS**

Art Director: Jay Johnson

Client: Colorado Cyclist

Medium: Oil on gessoed board

Size: 23" x 17"

263
Artist: **BART FORBES**

Art Director: Jack Scharr

Client: U.S. Olympic Committee

Medium: Oil on canvas

Size: 24" x 35"

260

261

262

263

264
Artist: **PAUL DAVIS**

Art Director: Paul Davis

Client: Bay Street Theatre

Medium: Acrylic, retouched and
altered in Photoshop on paper

Size: 14" x 11"

265
Artist: **C. F. PAYNE**

Art Director: Joe Pompeo

Agency: Saatchi & Saatchi

Client: Florida Citrus Growers

Medium: Oil, acrylic, watercolor,
colored pencil on board

Size: 13" x 11"

266
Artist: **GREGORY M. DEARTH**

Art Director: Scott Cooter

Agency: Ferrare Fleming

Client: PDC

Medium: Scratchboard

Size: 10" x 14"

267
Artist: **ROBERT CRAWFORD**

Art Director: Leon Kislowski

Agency: Bronner Slosberg & Humphrey

Client: IBM

Medium: Acrylic on masonite

Size: 17" x 10"

268
Artist: **ROBERT CRAWFORD**

Art Director: Brian Cox

Agency: Morgan & Partners

Client: Market Square

Medium: Acrylic on masonite

Size: 15" x 15"

264

265

266

267

268

269
Artist: **JOE SORREN**
Art Director: Sally Weigarten
Client: Heller Financial
Medium: Acrylic on canvas
Size: 29" x 24"

270
Artist: **JANET WOOLLEY**
Art Director: Chris Chaffin
Client: Hal Riney & Partners
Medium: Mixed
Size: 17" x 16"

271
Artist: **CYNTHIA VON BUHLER**
Art Director: Cozbi Sanchez-Cabrera
Client: Sony Records
Medium: Gouache on canvas and wood
Size: 24" x 24"

272
Artist: **RICK VALICENTI**
Art Director: Rick Valicenti
Client: Trek USA
Medium: Photography, digital,
film emulsion and pixels

273
Artist: **RICK VALICENTI**
Art Director: Rick Valicenti
Client: Gilbert Paper
Medium: Photography, digital,
film emulsion and pixels

269

270

271

272

273

274
Artist: **JOE SORREN**
Art Director: Holden Hume
Agency: Verb Communications
Client: Rossignol
Medium: Acrylic on canvas

275
Artist: **MARK ULRIKSEN**
Art Director: Shane Altman
Agency: The Richards Group
Client: Knows Cole Haan
Medium: Acrylic on paper
Size: 11" x 9"

276
Artist: **JAMES McMULLAN**
Art Director: Jim Russek
Agency: Russek Advertising
Client: Lincoln Center Theater
Medium: Gouache
Size: 14" x 8"

277
Artist: **PETER BOLLINGER**
Art Director: Doug Michaels
Agency: Michaels World
Client: Blue Star Inc.
Medium: SGI, Iris print
Size: 19" x 12"

278
Artist: **DAVID LANCE GOINES**
Art Director: David Lance Goines
Client: Sioux City Art Center
Medium: Photo-offset lithography
Size: 24" x 17"

274

275

276

277

278

279
Artist: **W.C. BURGARD**
Art Director: W.C. Burgard
Client: University Productions
Medium: Pastel on paper
Size: 17" x 11"

280
Artist: **DANIEL CRAIG**
Art Director: Sal Garguilo
Agency: Nappi Eliran Murphy
Client: New York City Opera
Medium: Acrylic on ragboard
Size: 23" x 15"

281
Artist: **DANIEL CRAIG**
Art Director: Sal Garguilo
Agency: Nappi Eliran Murphy
Client: New York City Opera
Medium: Acrylic on ragboard
Size: 24" x 15"

282
Artist: **DAVID LANCE GOINES**
Art Director: David Lance Goines
Client: Franciscan Estate Selections
Medium: Photo-offset lithography
Size: 24" x 17"

279

280

281

282

283
Artist: **ADAM NIKLEWICZ**
Art Director: Sal Garguilo
Agency: Nappi Eliran Murphy
Client: New York City Opera
Medium: Acrylic on gessoed board
Size: 16" x 12"

283A
Artist: **SCOTT McKOWEN**
Art Director: Doug Wager
Client: Arena Stage, Washington, DC
Medium: Scratchboard, scanned and
colorized digitally in Photoshop
Size: 8" x 5"

284
Artist: **JOHN P. MAGGARD**
Art Directors: Scott Hull
Frank Sturgis
Client: Scott Hull Assoc.
Medium: Oil, acrylic on Strathmore
Size: 18" x 12"

285
Artist: **AL HIRSCHFELD**
Art Director: Margo Feiden
Client: Castle Hill Productions
Medium: Pen & ink etching,
watercolor, lithography

283

283 A

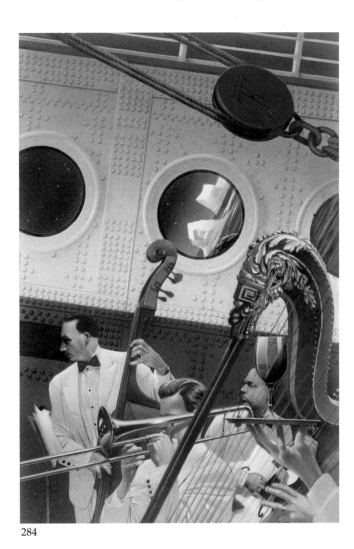

284

285

286
Artist: **GARY KELLEY**
Art Director: Risë Nathan
Client: Memphis Convention &
Visitors Bureau
Medium: Pastel on paper

287
Artist: **GARY KELLEY**
Art Director: Francine Kass
Client: W.W. Norton Co., Inc.
Medium: Pastel on paper
Size: 22" x 13"

288
Artist: **TED WRIGHT**
Art Director: Dwight Yoakam
Client: Reprise Records
Medium: Oil based silk-screen inks on
stone hinge rag paper
Size: 33" x 15"

289
Artist: **AL HIRSCHFELD**
Art Director: Margo Feiden
Client: Castle Hill Productions
Medium: Pen & ink etching, watercolor,
lithography

286

287

288

289

290
Artist: **PHILIPPE LARDY**
Art Director: Alain Lachartre
Client: Vue Sur La Ville
Medium: Gouache
Size: 14" x 11"

291
Artist: **PHILIPPE LARDY**
Art Director: Randy Lim
Client: Chateau Ste. Michelle
Medium: Gouache
Size: 10" x 22"

292
Artist: **PAUL ROGERS**
Art Director: Sal Garguillo
Agency: Nappi Eliran Murphy
Client: Big Apple Circus
Medium: Acrylic on board
Size: 26" x 15"

293
Artist: **MARCOS SORENSEN**
Medium: Digital, Photoshop, Iris print
Size: 10" x 8"

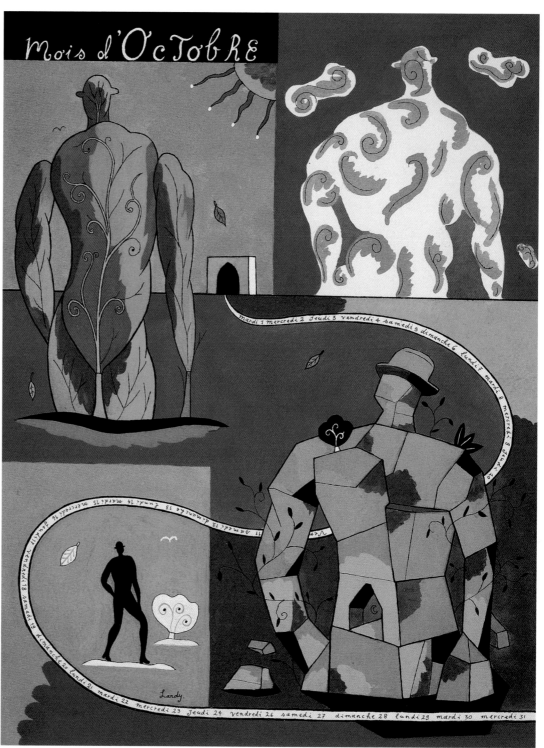

290

291

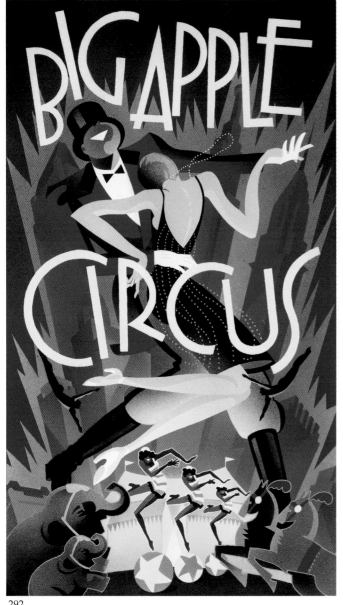

292

293

294
Artists: **ETIENNE DELESSERT**
GARY KELLEY

Art Director: Etienne Delessert

Client: Joseloff Gallery / University of
Connecticut

Medium: Watercolor, pastel

Size: 14" x 11"

295
Artist: **ETIENNE DELESSERT**

Art Director: Rita Marshall

Client: Les Fréres Ausoni

Medium: Acrylic on tin

Size: 20" x 18"

296
Artist: **JOE CIARDIELLO**

Art Directors: Tommy Steele
John O'Brien

Client: Capitol Records

Medium: Pen & ink, watercolor on paper

Size: 11" x 11"

297
Artist: **JOE CIARDIELLO**

Art Directors: Tommy Steele
John O'Brien

Client: Capitol Records

Medium: Pen & ink, watercolor on paper

Size: 10" x 10"

294

295

Amos Milburn

John Lee Hooker

298
Artist: **THEO RUDNAK**
Art Director: Theo Rudnak
Client: Renard Represents
Medium: Gouache on linen, ragboard

299
Artist: **JOHN RUSH**
Art Director: Ken Brockway
Agency: N. W. Ayer
Client: Zurich-American
    Insurance Group
Medium: Oil on canvas
Size: 13" x 40"

300
Artist: **POL TURGEON**
Art Director: Melinda Kanipe
Agency: Saatchi & Saatchi Pacific
Client: Toyota
Medium: Mixed, collage on paper
Size: 13" x 20"

301
Artist: **JAMES McMULLAN**
Client: HarperCollins/
    Michael di Capua Books
Medium: Watercolor
Size: 8" x 14"

298

299

This is Pol Turgeon's
RAV 4 dream.

Pol Turgeon, illustrator

300

301

302
Artist: **MARY FLOCK LEMPA**
Agency: Bartels & Co. Inc.
Medium: Scraper board, watercolor

303
Artist: **GIDEON KENDALL**
Art Director: Robert Fischer
Client: Geffen Records
Medium: Pen & ink with digital color
enhancement
Size: 6" x 6"

304
Artist: **DOUG JOHNSON**
Art Director: Doug Johnson
Client: Dodger Productions
Medium: Gouache on board
Size: 17" x 25"

305
Artist: **ISTVÁN OROSZ**
Art Director: Carolyn Hadlock
Client: Bingham Summers
Medium: Etching on paper
Size: 10" x 7"

306
Artist: **ISTVÁN OROSZ**
Art Director: Carolyn Hadlock
Client: Bingham Summers
Medium: Etching on paper
Size: 10" x 7"

302

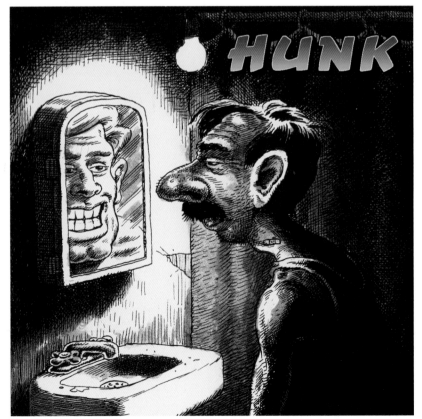

303

304

305

306

307
Artist: **ERIC WHITE**
Art Directors: B. Mossman
Eric White
Client: Sugarfix Records
Medium: Acrylic on board
Size: 14" x 14"

308
Artist: **HAYDN CORNNER**
Art Director: Loren Weeks
Agency: BLW & Associates
Client: Griggs-Anderson Research
Medium: Oil
Size: 10" x 15"

309
Artist: **CHARLES SANTORE**
Art Director: Don Bender
Client: Random House Value
Publishing, Inc.
Medium: Watercolor on Arches
Size: 13" x 20"

310
Artist: **CHRISTIAN CLAYTON**
Art Director: Greg Ross
Client: A&M Records
Medium: Acrylic, pencil, pen &
ink on paper
Size: 14" x 14"

307

308

309

310

311
Artist: **JIM SALVATI**

Art Director: Don Daly

Agency: Snowmass

Client: Hawaiian Pro Design

Medium: Xerox transfers, oil glaze on rag paper

Size: 8" x 9"

312
Artist: **KYLE RAETZ**

Art Director: Jodi Schwartz

Client: Espresso Royale Caffe Corporation

Medium: Digital, Adobe Illustrator on scraper board

Size: 20" x22"

313
Artist: **JAMES McMULLAN**

Art Director: Piper Murakami

Client: APL

Medium: Watercolor, gouache on paper

Size: 11" x 10"

314
Artist: **DENNIS ZIEMIENSKI**

Art Director: Pat Summers

Agency: Summer-McCann Inc.

Client: Salute to the Arts

Medium: Acrylic on canvas

311

312

313

314

315
Artist: **MARK ENGLISH**
Art Director: Tim Trabon
Client: Norman Rockwell Museum
Medium: Acrylic on canvas
Size: 22" x 17"

316
Artist: **SAM WARD**
Art Director: Charles Fillhardt
Client: Righteous Accelerator Boards
Medium: Digital, Macromedia Freehand
Size: 20" x 16"

317
Artist: **JOHN CARROLL DOYLE**
Art Director: John Carroll Doyle
Client: Blue Chicago
Medium: Oil on canvas

318
Artist: **MARY THELEN**
Art Director: Phil Silvestri
Agency: Messner Vetere Berger
McNamee
Client: MCI World
Medium: Color Aid silkscreened papers
on 2-ply vellum
Size: 18" x 23"

315

316

317

318

319

Artist: **LARRY McENTIRE**

Art Director: Leslie Singer

Client: Penguin USA

Medium: Acrylic on canvas

Size: 9" x 13"

320

Artist: **GARY BASEMAN**

Art Director: Azita Panaupour

Agency: Messner Vetere Berger McNamee

Client: International Paper

Medium: Acrylic on canvas

Size: 10" x 10"

321

Artist: **BILL MAYER**

Art Director: William Rabiro

Agency: Schell Mullaney Inc.

Client: Schell Mullaney Inc.

Medium: Dyes, gouache

Size: 11" x 14"

322

Artist: **DAVID O'KEEFE**

Art Director: Dan Cohen

Agency: Angotti, Thomas, Hedge, Inc.

Client: Fuji

Medium: Clay sculpture

Size: 13" x 11"

319

320

321

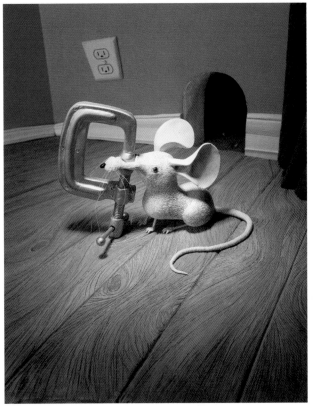

322

PAUL DAVIS, Chair
Illustrator/painter/graphic designer
Paul Davis Studio

MARC BURCKHARDT
Illustrator

ROCCO CALLARI
Art Director
United Nations

PINO DAENI
Illustrator

ANNE DIEBEL
Art Director
Clarion Books

ERIC DINYER
Illustrator

DEBORAH PARUOLO
City University of New York

KENNETH SMITH
Assistant Art Director
Time

RISA ZAITSCHEK
Art Director
Sony Music

INSTITUTIONAL

• •

Award
Winners

• • • • • • • • • • • • • • • • • • • •

MICHAEL DEAS
Gold Medal

JEFFREY DECOSTER
Gold Medal

ETIENNE DELESSERT
Gold Medal

FRED OTNES
Gold Medal

MICHELLE BARNES
Silver Medal

ANITA KUNZ
Silver Medal

ROBERT NEUBECKER
Silver Medal

323
Artist: **MICHAEL J. DEAS**
Art Director: Phil Jordan
Client: U.S. Postal Service
Medium: Oil on gessoed paper
Size: 5" x 9"

Institutional Gold Medal
MICHAEL DEAS
This painting, a portrait of the playwright Thornton Wilder, was commissioned by the U.S. Postal Service for use on a commemorative stamp issued in April 1997. The background depicts Grover's Corner, New Hampshire, the fictional setting for "Our Town." The artist has completed a half-dozen portraits for the Postal Service, including likenesses of Tennessee Williams, F. Scott Fitzgerald, and Marilyn Monroe. His portrait of James Dean won a Gold Medal from the Society of Illustrators in 1996.

324
Artist: **JEFFREY DECOSTER**
Medium: Acrylic
Size: 26" x 15"

Institutional Gold Medal
JEFFREY DECOSTER
"The evolution of my work, lately, has involved 'painting out' information and creating compositions with empty spaces. Concurrently, I have noticed an obsession with cleaning out my garage. I live in San Francisco and have done illustrations for magazines, CD covers, annual reports, and event posters. I go to a weekly drawing workshop and I teach at the California College of Arts and Crafts."

325
Artist: **ETIENNE DELESSERT**
Art Director: Rita Marshall
Client: Les Fréres Ausoni
Medium: Acrylic on tin
Size: 20" x 18"

Institutional Gold Medal
ETIENNE DELESSERT
For twenty-five years Etienne Delessert had been creating promotional posters for Les Frères Ausoni of Switzerland. From the onset they said, "No fashion, no models." Etienne began creating cats, which have now become the company's accepted trademark. The collected feline images have been exhibited in galleries and will soon be published in a book. Here he shows two generations--the mature, observing adult and the energetic yet naive youth. The relationship between sons and fathers is a topic the artist has often revisited. This acrylic is on tin which he finds absorbs more light when gessoed.

326
Artist: **FRED OTNES**
Art Director: John deCesare
Client: Reece Inc.
Medium: Mixed, collage
Size: 17" x 13"

Institutional Gold Medal
FRED OTNES
"For a number of years exploration into the potential applications of printmaking techniques, collage, and adaptation of photographic elements into my illustrations have been an area of investigation. The integration of unexpected elements juxtaposed with alien objects. The past and the future. Photo positives and negatives. The two-dimensional and the three. The abstract and the concrete. New processes, at least for me, are areas of development and experimentation."

327
Artist: **MICHELLE BARNES**

Art Director: Michelle Barnes

Client: Spiritus Music

Medium: Collage, acrylic on board

Size: 11" x 18"

Institutional Silver Medal
MICHELLE BARNES
A native of Colorado, Michelle Barnes was educated at Colorado State University and The School of Visual Arts. After a stint at a Parisian record company, she returned to New York to work for editorial clients. She has taught nationwide and conducted workshops in Tokyo, Japan, and Seoul, Korea. In 1992 she started "WIG," (Women Illustration Group) and curated a show of women illustrators held in Soho, New York. She is collaborating with Greg Spalenka on a book with a CD of original music. She is also working on 225 paintings for an interactive CD-ROM verison of the Bible.

328
Artist: **ANITA KUNZ**

Art Director: D.J. Stout

Client: Society of Illustrators

Medium: Watercolor, gouache on board

Size: 18" x 13"

Institutional Silver Medal
ANITA KUNZ

Born in Toronto, Canada, in 1956, Kunz graduated from The Ontario College of Art in 1978. She has since lived in London, New York, and Toronto, working for international magazines, book publishers, and advertising agencies. Using a combination of watercolors and gouache, she has produced critically acclaimed paintings which have been featured in graphics magazines internationally. She conducts workshops and gives lectures at universities and institutions, including the Smithsonian in Washington. Honored with many awards, her works are in the permanent collections at the Library of Congress and Musée Militaire de France in Paris.

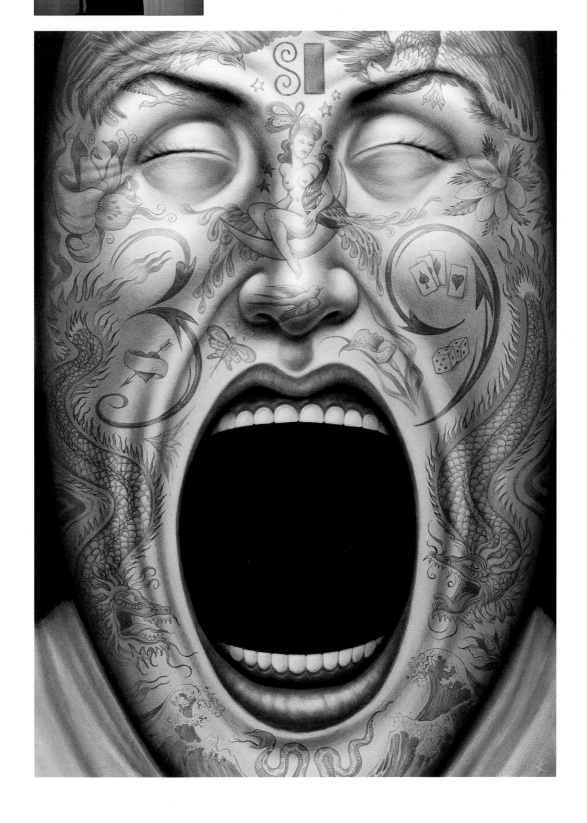

329
Artist: **ROBERT NEUBECKER**
Art Director: Linda Sullivan
Client: Brigham Young University
Medium: Acrylic, ink on Arches paper
Size: 15" x 11"

Institutional Silver Medal
ROBERT NEUBECKER
"I spent my formative years as an illustrator working for *The New York Times* where the picture-making philosophy was simple: substance over surface. Style can be a message in and of itself, but I prefer to work from the inside out, starting with the idea. Content is everything—clarity of message, storytelling. Technique or 'style' follows. The lawyer picture is about sophistry and skewing truth. I chose to paint it very roughly in acrylics to convey anger. Luckily, Linda Sullivan, my Art Director, trusted me and let me have total freedom. I love that."

330
Artist: **MICHAEL GARLAND**

Art Director: Kate Hixon

Client: NYNEX

Medium: Digial, Photoshop, PowerMac

Size: 10" x 14"

331
Artist: **BILL NELSON**

Art Directors: Bill Nelson
Jim Loehr

Client: Spectrum

Medium: Mixed, 3-dimensional sculpture

Size: 15" x 12"

332
Artist: **ALETHA REPPEL**

Art Director: Megan Barra

Client: Festival International de
Louisiane

Medium: Oil, wire screen, copper foil,
fabric on wood

Size: 35" x 20"

330

331

332

333
Artist: **ROBERT HUNT**
Art Director: Roger Carpenter
Client: Robert Hunt/ Kazu Sano
Medium: Oil on linen
Size: 23" x 38"

334
Artist: **MARK HESS**
Client: Newborn Group
Medium: Oil, acrylic on board
Size: 14" x 10"

335
Artist: **JAMES DIETZ**
Art Director: Bob Westervelt
Client: Spofford House
Medium: Oil on canvas
Size: 30" x 60"

336
Artist: **LINDA DEVITO SOLTIS**
Art Director: Jacqueline Dedell
Medium: Acrylic on linen canvas
Size: 17" x18"

333

334

335

336

337
Artist: **PAUL DAVIS**
Art Director: Silas Rhodes
Client: School of Visual Arts
Medium: Acrylic, collage on wood
Size: 12" x 9"

338
Artist: **WENDELL MINOR**
Art Director: JoAnn Losinger
Client: The Norman Rockwell Museum
Medium: Acrylic on canvas
Size: 24" x 36"

339
Artist: **PETER DE SÈVE**
Art Director: Bethante Deeney
Client: Graphic Artists Guild
Medium: Watercolor on paper
Size: 13" x 10"

340
Artist: **SEYMOUR CHWAST**
Art Director: Seymour Chwast
Client: AIGA/Cleveland
Medium: Colored pencil, acrylic on cardboard
Size: 16" x 13"

337

338

339

340

341
Artist: **MICHELLE BARNES**
Art Director: Michelle Barnes
Client: Atlanta Magazine
Medium: Mixed
Size: 14" x 10"

342
Artist: **MICHELLE BARNES**
Art Director: Michelle Barnes
Client: Spiritus Music
Medium: Collage, acrylic,
         oil pastel on board
Size: 6" x 19"

343
Artist: **BINA ALTERA**
Art Director: Hans Rueffert
Client: Zehrapushu, Inc.
Medium: Photo collage on wood
Size: 10" x 7"

344
Artist: **BINA ALTERA**
Art Director: Hans Rueffert
Client: Zehrapushu, Inc.
Medium: Photo collage on wood
Size: 10" x 7"

341

342

343

344

345
Artist: **MARTY BLAKE**
Medium: Collage
Size: 6" x 4"

346
Artist: **LYNN BYWATERS**
Client: Sunrise Publications
Medium: Gouache on Strathmore cold
     press paper
Size: 6" x 8"

347
Artist: **ROBERT NEUBECKER**
Art Director: Linda Sullivan
Client: Brigham Young University
Medium: Watercolor, ink, acrylic on
     Arches paper
Size: 12" x 9"

348
Artist: **LISA FALKENSTERN**
Medium: Oil on canvas
Size: 40" x 30"

345

346

317

348

349
Artist: **MARC BURCKHARDT**
Art Director: Ellen Elschlepp
Client: Doubleday Magazine
Medium: Acrylic on board
Size: 13" x 10"

350
Artist: **LORI ANZALONE**
Art Director: Michael Bierut
Agency: Pentagram
Client: Mohawk Paper Mills, Inc.
Medium: Acrylic, gouache on Letramax 5000
Size: 11" x 14"

351
Artist: **FRANK MARCHESE**
Client: Sloan McGill
Medium: Collage
Size: 20" x 16"

352
Artist: **PHILIPPE WEISBECKER**
Medium: Pencil
Size: 13" x 18"

349

350

351

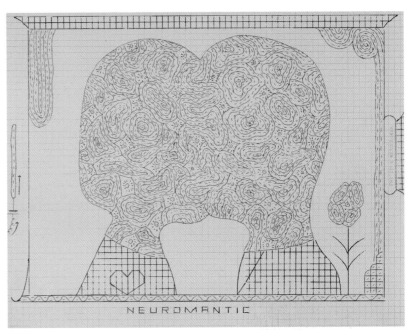

352

353
Artist: **LAURIE KELLER**
Art Director: Laurie Keller
Client: Hallmark Cards
Medium: Collage on chipboard
Size: 13" x 18"

354
Artist: **KAZUHIKO SANO**
Art Director: Roger Carpenter
Client: Society of Illustrators
Medium: Acrylic on textured museum board
Size: 17" x 33"

355
Artist: **JOEL NAKAMURA**
Art Director: Donna Bonavita
Client: KPMG
Medium: Acrylic, oil on tooled tin
Size: 9" x 15"

356
Artist: **JOHN CRAIG**
Art Director: Nadine Stellavato
Client: Level One
Medium: Engraving collage, digital color
Size: 9" x 9"

357
Artist: **JOHN CRAIG**
Art Director: Nadine Stellavato
Client: Level One
Medium: Engraving collage, digital color
Size: 9" x 9"

353

354

355

356

357

358
Artist: **BRAD HOLLAND**

Art Director: Joachin Beutler

Agency: H. F. & P.

Client: Haniel

Medium: Acrylic on masonite

Size: 17" x 14"

359
Artist: **CYNTHIA VON BUHLER**

Art Directors: Hans Rueffert
Clive Barker

Client: HarperCollins

Medium: Gouache on canvas with live
dove, wood, metal wire

Size: 40" x 30"

360
Artist: **DAN YACCARINO**

Client: Hartwick College

Medium: Alkyd on Bristol

Size: 15" x 10"

361
Artist: **JULIETTE BORDA**

Art Director: Eva Wojnar

Client: American Airlines

Medium: Gouache on paper

Size: 9" x 7"

362
Artist: **RICH BORGE**

Client: Alternative Pick and Day One

Medium: Wood, metal, polymer clay
collage. Assemblage scanned
and manipulated digitally.

Size: 9" x 9"

363
Artist: **RICH BORGE**

Art Directors: Bill Bowen
Jim Denk

Client: The Publications Co.

Medium: Wood, paper, wire, metal, oil.
Assemblage scanned and
manipulated digitally.

Size: 11" x 8"

358

359

360

Sixty tins of cat food Each day.

361

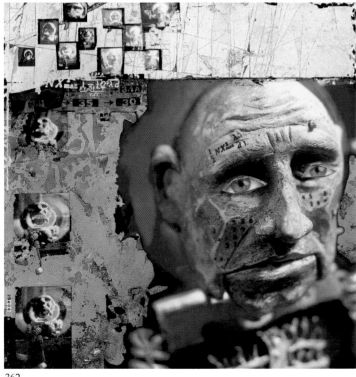

362

363

364
Artist: **GÜRBÜZ D. EKSIOGLU**

Art Director: Sally Heflin

Client: Self Promotion

Medium: Ink, watercolor

Size: 14" x 12"

365
Artist: **TERRY ALLEN**

Art Director: Craig Byers

Agency: Axis Communications

Client: Software AG

Medium: Airbrush on board

366
Artist: **SEYMOUR CHWAST**

Art Director: Seymour Chwast

Client: Mohawk Paper/Berman
Printing/Pushpin Group

Medium: Acrylic on canvas

Size: 18" x 28"

367
Artist: **SEYMOUR CHWAST**

Art Director: Seymour Chwast

Client: Mohawk Paper/Berman
Printing/The Pushpin Group

Medium: Acrylic on cardboard

Size: 11" x 9"

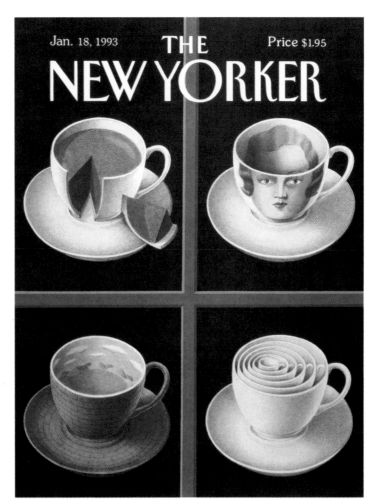

364

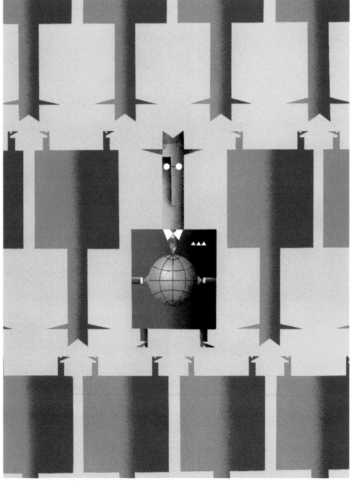

365

368
Artist: **MELISSA GRIMES**

Art Director: Scott Ray

Client: Dallas Society of Visual
Communications

Medium: Collage on poster board

369
Artist: **DAVID E. LESH**

Art Director: David Sibley

Client: Ameritrust

Medium: Mixed

Size: 9" x 7"

370
Artists: **JULIETTE BORDA**

Art Director: Lori Siebert

Client: Cincinnati's Contemporary
Arts Center

Medium: Gouache on paper

Size: 11" x 9"

371
Artist: **CRAIG FRAZIER**

Art Director: Craig Frazier

Client: The Energy Foundation

Medium: Cut film, Iris print

Size: 10" x 8"

368

369

370

371

372
Artist: **ELLEN WEINSTEIN**

Art Director: Gordon Jee

Client: Polygram Classics

Medium: Collage, butterfly on chipboard

Size: 10" x 10"

373
Artist: **CYNTHIA VON BUHLER**

Art Directors: Hans Rueffert
Clive Barker

Client: HarperCollins

Medium: Gouache on canvas with pig
heart on wood. Wood
construction by Xavier Dietrich

Size: 27" x 20"

374
Artist: **CYNTHIA VON BUHLER**

Art Directors: Hans Rueffert
Clive Barker

Client: HarperCollins

Medium: Gouache on canvas with bull-
frog skeleton on wood

Size: 36" x 20"

375
Artist: **WENDELL MINOR**

Art Director: Al Cetta

Client: HarperCollins

Medium: Acrylic on masonite

Size: 11" x 19"

372

373

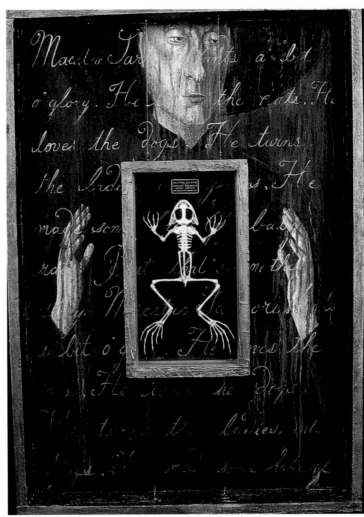

374

375

376
Artist: **DAN YACCARINO**
Medium: Cardboard, wood, acrylic on wood
Size: 15" x 16"

377
Artist: **EDEL RODRIGUEZ**
Medium: Mixed on paper
Size: 9" x 11"

378
Artist: **THORINA H. ROSE**
Client: Index Gallery, Osaka, Japan
Medium: Gouache on paper
Size: 9" x 12"

379
Artist: **LAURIE KELLER**
Art Director: Laurie Keller
Client: Hallmark Cards
Medium: Acrylic on chipboard
Size: 7" x 5"

376

377

378

379

380

Artist: **TERESA FASOLINO**

Art Director: Rocco Callari

Client: United Nations Postal Administration

Medium: Oil on canvas

Size: 8" x 36"

381

Artist: **TERESA FASOLINO**

Art Director: Rocco Callari

Client: United Nations Postal Administration

Medium: Oil on canvas

Size: 8" x 36"

382

Artist: **TERESA FASOLINO**

Art Director: Rocco Callari

Client: United Nations Postal Administration

Medium: Oil on canvas

Size: 8" x 36"

383

Artist: **THOMAS VAUGHAN**

Art Directors: Skip Leipke
Mark English

Medium: Acrylic, watercolor, oil, colored pencil on board

Size: 10" x 8"

384

Artist: **RICK VALICENTI**

Art Director: Rick Valicenti

Client: Gilbert Paper

Medium: Photography, digital, film emulsion and pixels

380

381

382

380 Detail

383

384

385

Artist: **KRISTEN BALOUCH**

Medium: Digital, Iris print

Size: 11" x 10"

386

Artist: **BILL NELSON**

Art Directors: Terry McCaffrey
  Howard Paine

Client: U.S. Postal Service

Medium: Colored pencil on matt board

Size: 5" x 6"

387

Artist: **BILL NELSON**

Art Directors: Terry McCaffrey
  Howard Paine

Client: U.S. Postal Service

Medium: Colored pencil on matt board

Size: 5" x 6"

388

Artist: **MICHAEL BARTALOS**

Art Director: Richard Sheaff

Client: United States Postal Service

Medium: Software: Adobe illustrator 6.0,
  Output: Iris print

Size: 8" x 5"

385

385 Detail

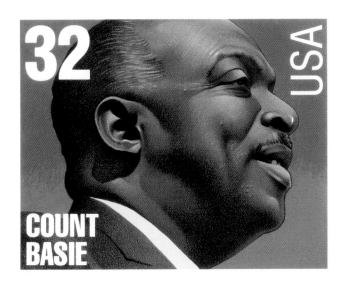

386

387

388

389
Artist: **ROBERT MEGANCK**
Medium: Oil on watercolor paper
Size: 17" x 20"

390
Artist: **PATRICK D. MILBOURN**
Art Director: Jean A. Coyne
Client: Communication Arts
Medium: Oil on ragboard
Size: 26" x 17"

391
Artist: **PATRICK D. MILBOURN**
Art Director: Jean A. Coyne
Client: Communication Arts
Medium: Oil on canvas board
Size: 16" x 20"

392
Artist: **RUSSELL McGONAGLE**
Client: Alternative Pick
Medium: Photo collage on photo paper
Size: 19" x 15"

389

390

391

392

393
Artist: **DAVE McKEAN**
Medium: Computer, Iris print

394
Artist: **GARY BASEMAN**
Art Director: Sherry Squier
Client: Louisville Graphic Design Assoc.
Medium: Acrylic on canvas
Size: 23" x 17"

395
Artist: **GARY BASEMAN**
Art Director: Laura Barnes
Client: CSCA
Medium: Acrylic on canvas
Size: 16" x 22"

396
Artist: **DAVE McKEAN**
Medium: Computer, Iris print

393

394

395

397
Artist: **REGAN TODD DUNNICK**
Medium: Acrylic on board
Size: 9" x 5"

398
Artist: **BART FORBES**
Client: Ussery Printing Co.
Medium: Oil on canvas
Size: 19" x 16"

399
Artist: **JOSEPH DANIEL FIEDLER**
Client: The Black Book
Medium: Alkyd on Strathmore
Size: 8" x 8"

400
Artist: **SAM WARD**
Art Director: Beth Lankes
Client: Security Management Magazine
Medium: Gouache on Bristol board coated with acrylic matte medium
Size: 16" x 12"

397

398

399

400

401
Artist: **KATHERINE LANDIKUSIC**
Art Director: Fayrol Unverferth
Client: Hallmark Cards
Medium: Pastel on paper
Size: 11" x 10"

402
Artist: **KATHERINE LANDIKUSIC**
Art Director: Fayrol Unverferth
Client: Hallmark Cards
Medium: Pastel on paper
Size: 11" x 15"

403
Artist: **KATHERINE LANDIKUSIC**
Art Director: Fayrol Unverferth
Client: Hallmark Cards
Medium: Pastel on paper

404
Artist: **DAVID SHANNON**
Art Director: David Shannon
Client: Scholastic
Medium: Acrylic on board
Size: 22" x 17"

401

402

403

404

405
Artist: **ETIENNE DELESSERT**
Art Director: Rita Marshall
Client: Les Fréres Ausoni
Medium: Acrylic on tin
Size: 20" x 14"

406
Artist: **ETIENNE DELESSERT**
Art Director: Rita Marshall
Client: Les Fréres Ausoni
Medium: Acrylic on tin
Size: 20" x 18"

407
Artist: **MARCO VENTURA**
Art Director: Sarah Hollander
Client: Mortgage Banking
Medium: Oil on paper
Size: 11" x 8"

408
Artist: **RAFAL OLBINSKI**
Art Director: Jessica Weber
Client: Juilliard School of Music
Medium: Acrylic on canvas

409
Artist: **ETIENNE DELESSERT**
Art Director: Rita Marshall
Client: Les Fréres Ausoni
Medium: Acrylic on tin
Size: 20" x 18"

405

406

407

408

409

410
Artists: **CHERYL GRIESBACH**
STANLEY MARTUCCI

Art Directors: Tom Egner
Stanley Martucci

Client: American Showcase

Medium: Oil on masonite

Size: 11" x 7"

411
Artist: **MICHAEL GIBBS**

Art Director: Linda Berns

Client: U.S. Generating Co.

Medium: Acrylic, Photoshop 3.0,
PowerMac, Iris print

Size: 14" x 9"

412
Artist: **ROBERT GIUSTI**

Art Director: Joan Sigman

Client: The Newborn Group

Medium: Acrylic on linen

413
Artist: **MARK HESS**

Medium: Acrylic on canvas

Size: 15" x 15"

410

411

412

413

414
Artist: **POLLY BECKER**
Art Director: John Tan
Client: John Tan
Medium: Mixed
Size: 8" x 10"

145
Artist: **POLLY BECKER**
Art Director: Ronn Campisi
Client: Federal Reserve Bank of Boston
Medium: Mixed
Size: 7" x 8"

416
Artist: **GARY BASEMAN**
Art Directors: Frank Viva
Randell Pearson
Client: YMCA Annual Report
Medium: Acrylic on canvas and paper
Size: 17" x 13"

417
Artist: **POLLY BECKER**
Art Director: Carol Dietrich
Client: Bloomberg
Medium: Mixed
Size: 8" x 10"

414

415

416

417

418
Artist: **PHILIPPE WEISBECKER**
Art Director: Frank Viva
Client: Butterfield & Robinson
Medium: Mixed
Size: 12" x 12"

419
Artist: **PHILIPPE WEISBECKER**
Art Director: Frank Viva
Client: Butterfield & Robinson
Medium: Mixed
Size: 12" x 12"

420
Artist: **RUSS WILSON**
Art Director: Bernard Michael Urban
Agency: Anson & Stoner
Client: Bagel Boulevard
Medium: Pastel on paper
Size: 15" x 19"

421
Artist: **RUSS WILSON**
Art Director: Bernard Michael Urban
Agency: Anson & Stoner
Client: Bagel Boulevard
Medium: Pastel on paper
Size: 15" x 19"

418

419

420

421

422
Artist: **DAVID WILCOX**
Art Director: Sue Baiie
Client: Tyco Labs
Medium: Acrylic on board

423
Artist: **DAVID WILCOX**
Art Director: Karen Lucas-Hardy
Client: The Newborn Group
Medium: Vinyl, acrylic on board
Size: 21" x 18"

424
Artist: **DAVID WILCOX**
Art Director: Chris Passehl
Client: Keiler & Co.
Medium: Vinyl, acrylic on board
Size: 15" x 14"

425
Artist: **DAVE CUTLER**
Art Director: Lester Ing
Agency: Foote, Cone & Belding
Client: Netcom
Medium: Acrylic on watercolor paper
Size: 10" x 8"

422

423

424

425

426
Artist: **PHILIPPE LARDY**
Art Director: Sandy Kauffman
Client: NYU
Medium: Gouache
Size: 13" x 10"

427
Artist: **PAUL ZWOLAK**
Client: Baltimore Gas and Electric
Company
Medium: Acrylic on canvas
Size: 18" x 14"

428
Artist: **DAVID E. LESH**
Art Director: Bob Kellerman
Client: American Superconductor
Medium: Mixed
Size: 12" x 8"

429
Artist: **PHILIPPE LARDY**
Art Director: Sandy Kauffman
Client: NYU
Medium: Gouache
Size: 13" x 10"

430
Artist: **JEFF FOSTER**
Art Director: Etta Wilkins
Medium: Acrylic on board
Size: 16" x 11"

426

427

428

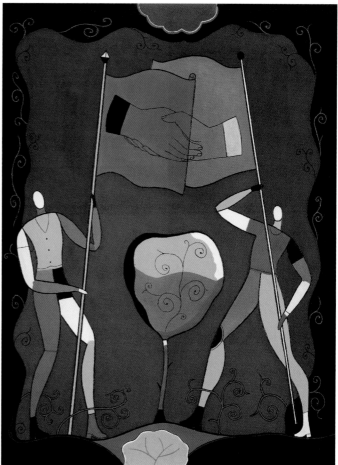

429

430

431

Artist: **JON ELLIS**

Client: American Showcase

Medium: Acrylic, assemblage circus memerobilia

Size: 14" x 20"

432

Artist: **PHIL BOATWRIGHT**

Client: The Alternative Pick`

Medium: Oil, acrylic on Strathmore, mounted on plywood

Size: 14" x 8"

433

Artist: **WARD SUTTON**

Art Director: Barry Ament

Client: Amesbros / Pearl Jam

Medium: Silk-screen on paper

Size: 21" x 15"

434

Artist: **WARD SUTTON**

Client: Art Rock

Medium: Silk-screen on paper

Size: 20" x 15"

435

Artist: **CLIFF NIELSEN**

Art Director: Chris Carter

Client: Topps

Medium: Computer, Iris print

Size: 19" x 14"

436

Artist: **CLIFF NIELSEN**

Art Director: Chris Carter

Client: Topps

Medium: Computer, Iris print

Size: 19" x 14"

431

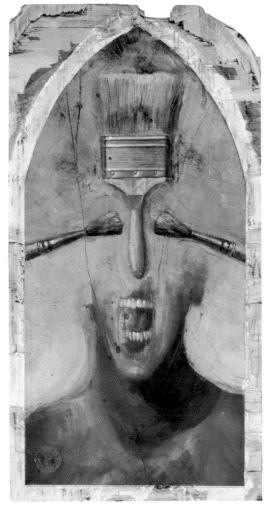

432

433

434

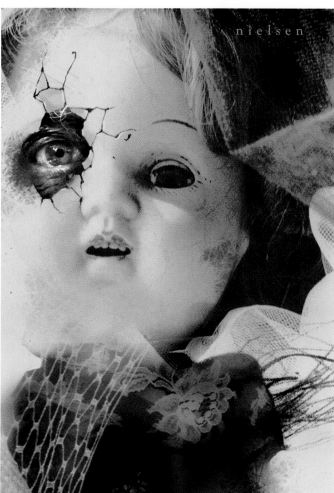

435

436

437
Artist: **JEFFREY FISHER**
Art Director: Nancy Hoefig
Client: Landor Associates
Medium: Acrylic
Size: 12" x 9"

438
Artist: **PAUL DAVIS**
Art Director: Paul Davis
Client: Acadiana Advertising
Medium: Acrylic on board
Size: 12" x 9"

439
Artists: **JULIETTE BORDA**
Art Director: Lori Siebert
Client: Cincinnati's Contemporary
	Arts Center
Medium: Gouache on paper
Size: 11" x 9"

440
Artist: **PAUL DAVIS**
Art Director: Bill Freeland
Client: City University of New York
Medium: Acrylic, collage on board
Size: 12" x 10"

437

438

439

440

441
Artist: **JORDIN ISLIP**
Art Director: Joe Gilbert
Client: Rhode Island School of Design
Medium: Mixed on paper
Size: 37" x 34"

442
Artist: **JORDIN ISLIP**
Art Director: David Armario
Client: Stanford Medicine/Stanford
  University
Medium: Mixed on paper
Size: 23" x 17"

443
Artist: **JORDIN ISLIP**
Medium: Mixed on paper
Size: 22" x 16"

444
Artist: **THOM ANG**
Art Director: John D'Agostino
Client: 20th Century Fox Home
  Entertainment
Medium: Collage, photography,
  acrylic on paper

441

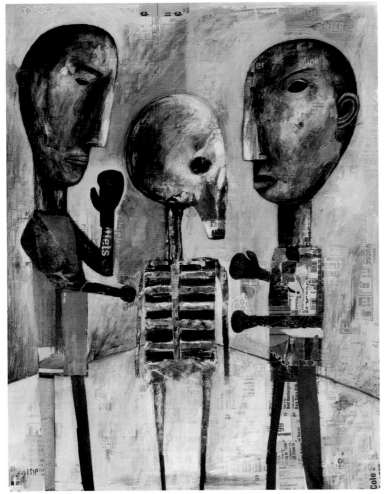

442

443

444

445
Artist: **JACQUI MORGAN**
Art Director: Jurek Wajdowicz
Client: UNIFEM
Medium: Transparent watercolor, computer on Arches paper

446
Artist: **NANETTE BIERS**
Art Director: Andy Dreyfus
Agency: CKS Partners
Client: APL Limited
Medium: Oil on canvas
Size: 19" x 17"

447
Artist: **RAFAL OLBINSKI**
Client: Nahan Galleries
Medium: Acrylic on canvas
Size: 31" x 21"

448
Artist: **MARK ENGLISH**
Art Director: Tim Trabon
Client: Trabon Printing
Medium: Acrylic on board

449
Artist: **ANDREW POWELL**
Client: Linda Henneman
Client: Pillsbury
Medium: Acrylic, collage, pencil, pastel on Rives BFK
Size: 20" x 16"

445

446

447

448

449

450

Artist: **FRED OTNES**

Art Director: John deCesare

Client: Reece Inc.

Medium: Mixed, collage on linen

Size: 24" x 19"

451

Artist: **FRED OTNES**

Art Director: John deCesare

Client: Reece Inc.

Medium: Mixed, collage

Size: 24" x 27"

452

Artist: **FRED OTNES**

Art Director: John deCesare

Client: Reece Inc.

Medium: Mixed, collage on linen

Size: 27" x 30"

453

Artist: **ROBERT NEUBECKER**

Art Director: Nancy Butkus

Client: Yale University Alumni Magazine

Medium: Watercolor, ink, acrylic on Arches paper

Size: 10" x 10"

450

451

452

453

454
Artist: **CATHLEEN TOELKE**
Art Director: David Hemsi
Client: American Academy of
Ophthalmology
Medium: Gouache on watercolor board
Size: 19" x 7"

455
Artist: **MARK ENGLISH**
Art Director: Piper Murakami
Client: APL
Medium: Pastel
Size: 16" x 14"

456
Artist: **RAÚL COLÓN**
Art Director: Susan Overstreet
Client: Arizona Theatre Co.
Medium: Watercolor, colored pencils,
litho pencils, "etched" on paper
Size: 12" x 11"

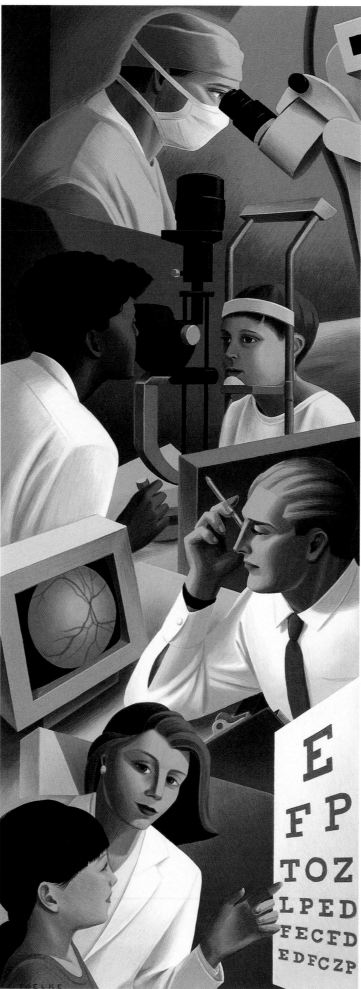

454

455

456

RAÚL COLÓN
Illustrator

KINUKO Y. CRAFT
Illustrator

ANITA KUNZ
Illustrator

KARL STEINBRENNER
Art Director
Steinbrenner & Company

INTERNATIONAL

457
Artist: **DIEGO HERRERA (YAYO)**
Art Director: Andrée Lauzon
Client: ClinD'oeil Magazine
Medium: Ink
Size: 27cm x 20cm

458
Artist: **MALIN LINDGREN**
Art Director: Susanne Andrée
Client: Sexton 87 Advertising Agency
Medium: Water-soluble oils
Size: 33cm x 47cm

459
Artist: **JÚRGEN MICK**
Client: Self promotion
Medium: Colored pencil
Size: 30cm x 33cm

460
Artist: **JÚRGEN MICK**
Client: Self promotion
Medium: Colored pencil
Size: 34cm x 41cm

461
Artist: **BERNARD LEDUC**
Size: 25cm x 45cm

462
Artist: **RICARDO MARTÍNEZ**
Art Director: Carmelo Caderot
Client: El Mundo
Medium: Scratchboard
Size: 21cm x 29cm

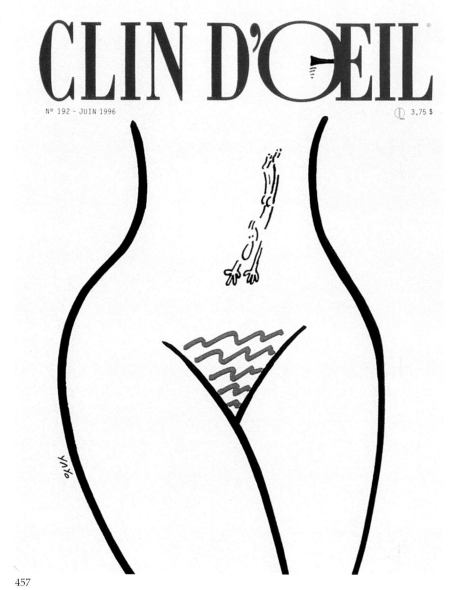

457

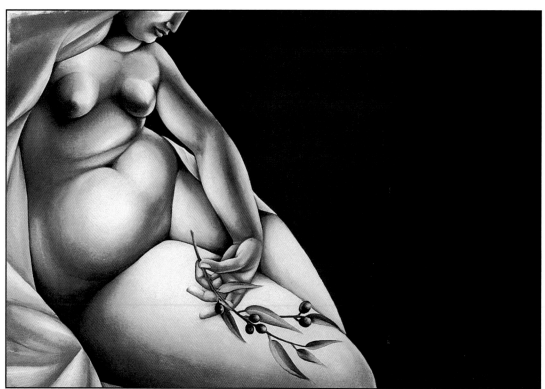

458

459

460

461

462

463
Artist: **ALAIN MASSICOTTE**
Medium: Acrylic sublimation print
Size: 37cm x 28cm

464
Artist: **ERIKO NAGASAWA**
Client: Central
Medium: Acrylic, gouache
Size: 390cm x 570cm

465
Artist: **MALIN LINDGREN**
Art Director: John Hamilton
Client: Reed Consumer Books
Medium: Water-soluble oils
Size: 25cm x 38cm

466
Artist: **KEVIN HAUFF**
Art Director: Rick Goodale
Client: Artbank International
Medium: Acrylic on canvas
Size: 80cm x 60cm

467
Artist: **HIDEKI MABUCHI**
Art Director: Masakazu Tanabe
Client: Space Prism
Medium: Acrylic on board
Size: 51cm x 36cm

468
Artist: **BRIDGET OHLSSON**
Art Director: Leonie Stot
Client: Penguin Books, Australia
Medium: Oil on canvas
Size: 23cm x 17cm

463

464

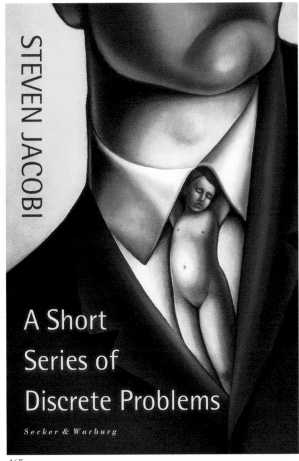

465

466

467

468

469
Artist: **ELZBIETA MURAWSKY**
Art Director: Elzbieta Murawsky
Client: KAW
Medium: Gouache
Size: 27cm x 14cm

470
Artist: **ALAIN PILON**
Art Director: Carmen Dunjko
Client: Saturday Night Magazine
Medium: Mixed

471
Artist: **SIGURBORG STEFÁNSDÓTTIR**
Art Directors: Áslaug Jõnsdottir
           Sigurborg Stefánsdóttir
Client: Mâlog Menning
Medium: Cut paper
Size: 21cm x 30cm

472
Artist: **HISAKO NAKAYAMA**
Art Director: Hisako Nakayama
Client: Space Prism
Size: 1030cm x 728cm

473
Artist: **HIDEKI MABUCHI**
Art Director: Masakazu Tanabe
Client: Central
Medium: Acrylic on board
Size: 57cm x 39cm

474
Artist: **JONATHAN MILNE**
Art Directors: Paul Madeley
Photographer: Henry Tregillis
Client: Zurich Commercial Insurance
Medium: Paper sculpture
Size: 80cm x 70cm

469

470

471

HISAKO NAKAYAMA POSTER EXHIBITION JUNE 13-18, 1996.
SPACE PRISM AM11:00~PM7:00 LAST PM5:00, 3F MATSUI BLDG, 1-2-26, HIGASHISAKURA, HIGASHI-KU, NAGOYA 461, PHONE 052-963-1829

472

473

474

475

Artist: **POL TURGEON**

Art Director: Bob Hambley

Client: World Wildlife Fund, Canada

Medium: Mixed

Size: 32cm x 23cm

476

Artist: **KIYOKA YAMAZUKI**

Size: 15cm x 10cm

477

Artist: **HIROSHI YOSHII**

Art Director: Toru Yuki

Client: Mainichi
        Communications Co., Ltd.

Medium: Computer

Size: 2587 pixels x 4052 pixels

478

Artist: **RICK SEALOCK**

Art Director: Rick Sealock

Client: Piglet Press

Medium: Mixed

Size: 46cm x 60cm

479

Artist: **ULISES CULEBRO**

Art Director: Carmelo Caderot

Client: El Mundo

Size: 32cm x 21cm

480

Artist: **HASHIMOTO YOSHINORI**

Art Director: Kazuhiro Tada

Client: Spoon Co., Ltd.

Size: 45cm x 25cm

475

476

477

478

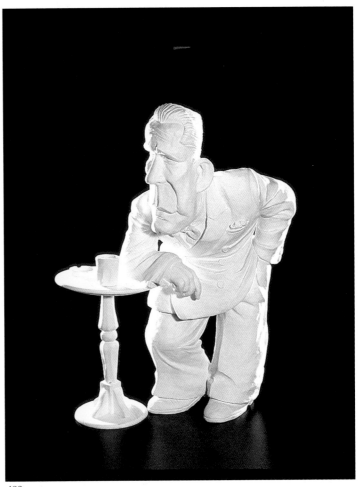

481
Artist: **RICK SEALOCK**
Art Director: Anders Knudsen
Client: Avenue Magazine
Medium: Mixed
Size: 37cm x 24cm

482
Artist: **RICARDO MARTÍNEZ**
Art Director: Carmelo Caderot
Client: El Mundo
Medium: Scratchboard
Size: 56cm x 31cm

483
Artist: **JAMES MARSH**
Art Director: Susan Buchanan
Client: Prospect Magazine
Medium: Acylic on canvas
Size: 28cm x 35cm

484
Artist: **HITOSHI MIURA**
Art Director: Hitoshi Miura
Client: Miura Creation
Size: 103cm x 73cm

485
Artist: **JOSEPH SALINA**
Art Director: Sara Tyson,
          James Ireland Design
Client: Ontario Naturalists Federation
Medium: Acrylic
Size: 45cm x 35cm

486
Artist: **KUNIO SATO**
Client: Nagoya Cable Network
Size: 23cm x 21cm

487
Artist: **GENEVIÈVE CÔNTÉ**
Art Director: Susan Meingast
Client: Healthwatch Magazine
Medium: Mixed
Size: 23cm x 33cm

481

482

483

484

485

486

487

488
Artist: **MIKI ISHII**
Art Director: Ryoichi Shiraishi
Client: Shueisha
Medium: Mixed, collage on board
Size: 45cm x 27cm

489
Artist: **JAEEUN CHOI**
Art Director: Jaeeun Choi
Client: Hanyang University
Medium: Acrylic
Size: 15cm x 24cm

490
Artist: **JOMA**
Art Director: Joan Corbera
Client: La Vanguardia
Size: 17cm x 13cm

491
Artist: **JOSEPH SALINA**
Art Director: David Woodside
Client: Financial Post Magazine
Medium: Acrylic
Size: 45cm x 37cm

492
Artist: **KOBRA EBRAHIMI**
Client: Soroush Press
Medium: Watercolor and ink
Size: 35cm x 20cm

493
Artist: **URS JOSEPH KNOBEL**
Client: House Advertising
Medium: Acrylic on linen
Size: 80cm x 100cm

488

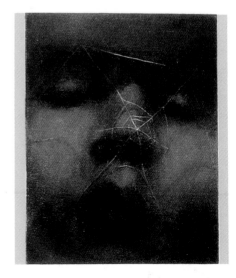

489

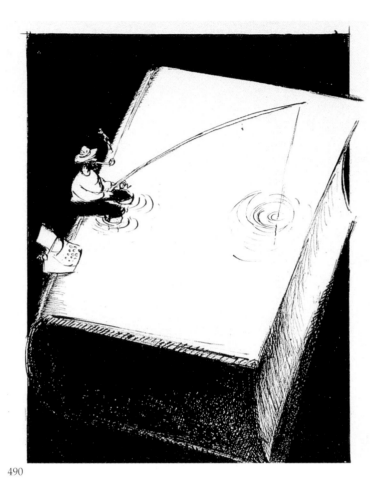

490

491

492

493

494

Artist: **ANDREJ AND OLGA DUGIN**

Art Director: Mathias Berg

Client: Esslinger Verlag

Medium: Watercolor on paper

Size: 27cm x 37cm

495

Artist: **ANDREJ AND OLGA DUGIN**

Art Director: Mathias Berg

Client: Esslinger Verlag

Medium: Watercolor on paper

Size: 21cm x 37cm

496

Artist: **MURRAY KIMBER**

Art Director: Glen Swale

Client: Tom Capital & Associates

Medium: Oil on canvas

Size: 165cm x 240cm

497

Artist: **MURRAY KIMBER**

Art Director: Murray Kimber

Client: David DiPaulo

Medium: Oil on canvas

Size: 90cm x 120cm

498

Artist: **RAÚL CRUZ FIGUEROA**

Art Director: Raúl Cruz Figueroa

Client: Gallito Comics Magazine

Size: 66cm x 51cm

499

Artist: **MIKI ISHII**

Art Director: Junko Sakakibara

Client: Winds Publications

Medium: Mixed, collage on board

Size: 36cm x 26cm

494

495

496

497

498

499

NEW VISIONS

The Society of Illustrators is once again proud to reproduce the catalogue of its Annual Student Scholarship Competition in this year's Annual Book so that you may see illustration from the perspective of these talented young artists.

Over 5,200 entries were received from 83 accredited institutions nationwide, from which 99 works by young artists were selected by a prestigious jury. Patrick Milbourn was instrumental in the crucial fund raising for awards, and Tim O'Brien, Chairman of the Education Committee, guided the jury through the lengthy selection process. The original works were exhibited at the Society of Illustrators Museum of American Illustration.

We are grateful to the many individuals, foundations, and organizations who contribute to the Scholarship Fund each year; their generous gifts support the bright futures of these worthy students. Contributors are listed in the following pages of "New Visions."

Exceptional craftsmanship and a high level of conceptual excitement are boldly present in the works of the young artists catalogued here. They are poised to enter the competitive world of illustration and are bound to succeed.

NEW VISIONS

"In 1984 I attended the awards ceremony for the Society of Illustrators Student Competition. The student work was exceptional, paintings created by illustration masters graced the walls of the Society and cutting edge contempories were joining the ranks. The following year, when a piece of mine was selected for the competition, I felt a surge of confidence. I began to believe I had what it took to be a free-lance illustrator. My affiliation with the Society reflects my own personal belief that it's never a mistake to maintain the highest possible standards and to associate with those who do the same."

Born in Pawtucket, RI, Begin attended Rhode Island School of Design, where she is currently teaching in the Illustration Department. She has been illustrating professionally since 1985 and has appeared in several Society of Illustrators Annuals, she won the Stevan Dohanos Award in 1995. Maryjane is represented by Jerry Leff Associates. Some clients include: Milton Bradley, William Morrow & Co., McDonalds, Johnson & Johnson, Putnam Publishing Group, Pillsbury, Proctor & Gamble, Disney, The Danbury Mint, Sesame Street Magazine, Little Brown & Co., and The Discovery Channel.

Maryjane Begin

"For anyone beginning in the business of illustration, the Society of Illustrators offers the best opportunity for exposure to potential clients. After having my work exhibited at the Society's Student Show in 1985. I received my first professional job from Golf Magazine, and I'm happy to say that I still work for them today."

Born in Absecon, New Jersey, Bennett attended Buck County Community College in Pennsylvania and School of Visual Arts in NYC, where he became an instructor in 1991. He has been illustrating professionally since 1986 and has appeared in several Society of Illustrators Annuals. James is represented by Richard Solomon. Some clients include: Golf, Forbes, TIME, MAD, Milton Bradley, Arista Records, Coca-Cola, Avon Books and Sprint.

James Robert Bennett

"The Society of Illustrators has always been a symbol of high standards and excellence. Being recognized by an institution with such a prestigious history validated my creative potential and encouraged me as a young artist."

Born in Arcadia, California and studied at Saddleback, Orange Coast and Art Center College. His works are mainly in the editorial field for clients such as Fortune, PC, Rolling Stone, Texas Monthly, Playboy and others. He has received awards from the Society's Annuals and CA and has been featured in Print and other trade publications. He recently collaborated with Michelle Barnes on "The Visions of Vesperina" a multidimensional concept of text, art, graphics and music.

Greg Spalenka

HALLMARK CORPORATE FOUNDATION
MATCHING GRANTS

The Hallmark Corporate Foundation of Kansas City, Missouri, is again this year supplying full matching grants for all of the awards in the Society's Student Scholarship Competition. Grants, restricted to the Illustration Departments, are awarded to the following institutions:

10,000	Art Center College of Design
6,500	School of Visual Arts
3,000	Paier College of Art
3,000	Pratt Institute
2,000	Academy of Art College
2,000	Fashion Institute of Technology
2,000	San Jose State University
1,500	Kutztown University
1,000	University of Arizona
1,000	California College of Arts & Crafts
1,000	University of Hartford
1,000	Savannah College of Art & Design
1,000	University of the Arts

SCHOLARSHIP COMMITTEE AND JURY

Committee
Tim O'Brien, Chair, Florian Bachelda (*New York Magazine*), Michael Deas
Donato Giancola, Ralph Giguere (*University of the Arts*)

Jury
N. Ascencios, Syndi Becker, (*American Health Magazine*), Steve Brennan,
Mirium Campiz (*M. Campiz Design*), Kinuko Craft, Steve Ellis, Eric Fowler,
Mary GrandPre, KAZ, Jerry LoFaro, Dave Matt (*Premiere Magazine*), Mel Odom,
Michael Picon (*Entertainment Weekly*), Edel Rodriguez (*TIME*), John Rush,
Mel Sanchez (*Marvel Comics*), Dave Stevenson (*Ballantine Books*),
Mark Summers, Greg Voth

Kadir Nelson
David Passalacqua, Instructor
Pratt Institute
$3,000 Jellybean Photographics Award
1998 "Call for Entries" Poster Award

Patrick Kochakji
David Mocarski, Instructor
Art Center College of Design
$2,500 The Starr Foundation Award

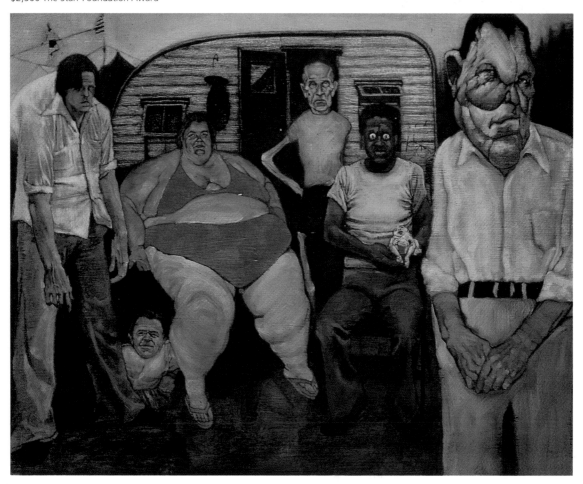

David Sean SanAngelo
Robert Zappalorti, Instructor
Paier College of Art
$3,000 Robert H. Blattner Award
Scholastic, Inc. Publication Award

Charlie Park
Linda Shepard, Instructor
Art Center College of Design
$2,500 The Starr Foundation Award

Thomas Starnes
Zhaoming Wu, Instructor
Academy of Art College
$2,000 The Franklin Mint
Foundation for the Arts
Award

Peter A. Krein
John Thompson, Instructor
Syracuse University
RSVP Directory Publication Award

Alfredo Mercado
Jim Salvati, Instructor
Art Center College of Design
$2,000 The Norman Rockwell Museum at Stockbridge Award

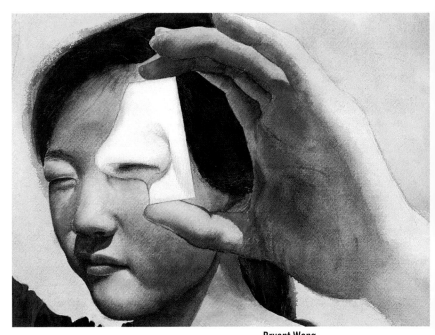

Bryant Wang
John Clapp, Instructor
San Jose State University
$2,000 Albert Dorne Award

Medgett
Morton Kaish, Instructor
Fashion Institute of Technology
$2,000 Albert Dorne Award

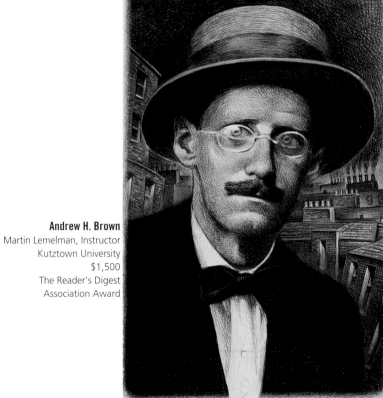

Andrew H. Brown
Martin Lemelman, Instructor
Kutztown University
$1,500
The Reader's Digest
Association Award

John Urso
Teresa Fasolino, Instructor
School of Visual Arts
$1,500 Jellybean Photographics Award

zu Ishihara
sa Desimini, Instructor
hool of Visual Arts
,500 Jellybean Photographics Award

Gennaro Capasso
Marvin Mattelson, Instructor
School of Visual Arts
$1,500 The Reader's Digest Association Award

Barry Appell
Mark Tocchet, Instructor
University of the Arts
$1,000 Norma and Alvin Pimsler Award

Steve Klamm
Frances Jetter, Instructor
School of Visual Arts
$1,000 Award
in Memory of Harry Rosenbaum

Seth Engstrom
Jim Salvati, Instructor
Art Center College of Design
$1,000 The Norman Rockwell Museum at Stockbridge Award

John Hermanowski Jr.
Marvin Mattelson, Instructor
School of Visual Arts
$1,000 Friends of the
Institute of
Commercial Art
Award

John Copeland
Susan Gross, Instructor
California College of
Arts & Crafts
$1,000 Dick Blick
Art Materials Award

Walter O'Neal
David Mocarski, Instructor
Art Center College of Design
$1,000 Award in Memory of Augie Napoli

Edward Shaw
Eve Olitsky, Instructor
University of Hartford
$1,000 Award in Memory of Meg Wohlberg

Adam Rex
David Christiana, Instructor
University of Arizona
$1,000 Award
in Memory of Fred
Peterson

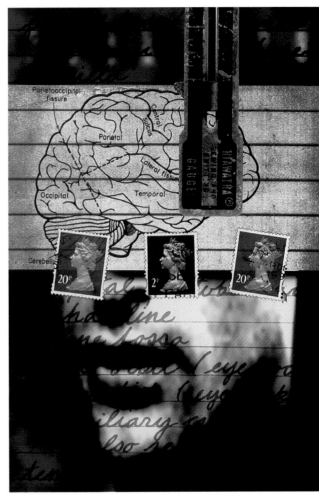

Jason Statts
Durwin Talon, Instructor
Savannah College of Art & Design
$1,000 Award in Memory of Herman Lambert

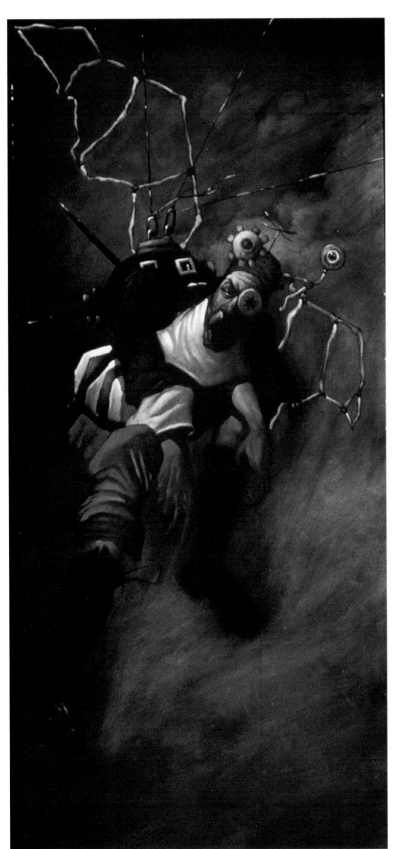

Francisco Valverde
David Mocarski, Instructor
Art Center College of Design
$1,000 Kirchoff/Wohlberg Award
in Memory of Francis Means

2

1

3

7

8

5

6

9

15

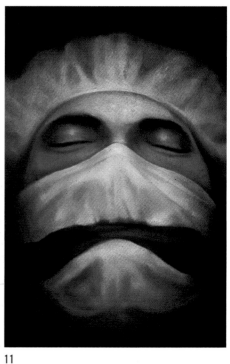

11

13

14

12

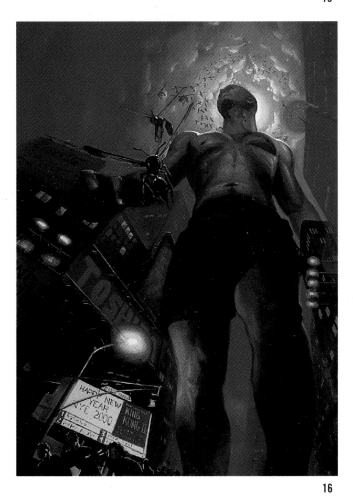

16

10

20

19

22

24

18

21

17

23

THE EXHIBIT

30

27

32

29

25

26

31

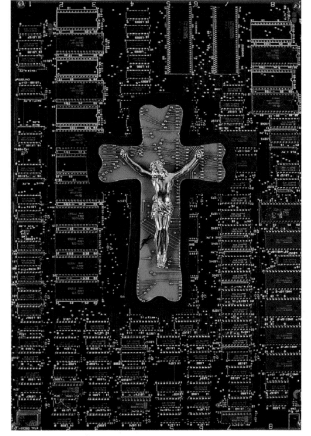

28

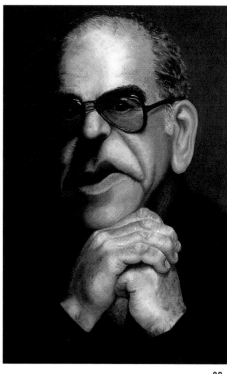

36

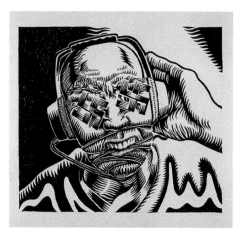

33

38

37

39

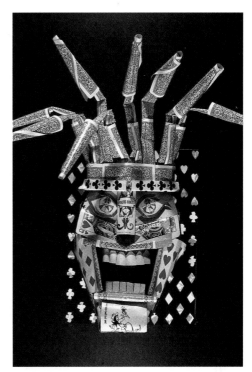

34

35

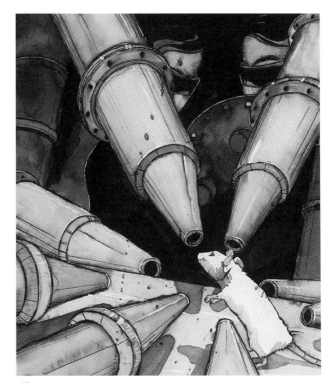

40

THE EXHIBIT

43

47   42

45

46

48

41

44

THE EXHIBIT

50

51

53

52

54

49

57

56

55

60

58

63

61

65

64

66

59

62

THE EXHIBIT

70

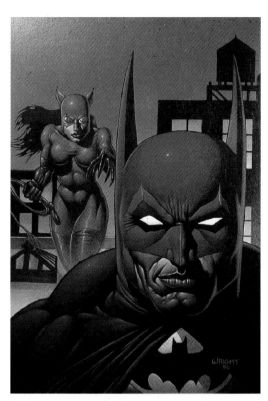

73

72

69

74

68

71

75

67

ARTIST INDEX

ARTIST INDEX

ARTIST INDEX

ARTIST INDEX

ARTIST INDEX

INTERNATIONAL ARTIST INDEX

ART DIRECTORS, CLIENTS, AGENCIES

ART DIRECTORS, CLIENTS, AGENCIES

INTERNATIONAL ART DIRECTORS, CLIENTS, AGENCIES

PROFESSIONAL STATEMENTS

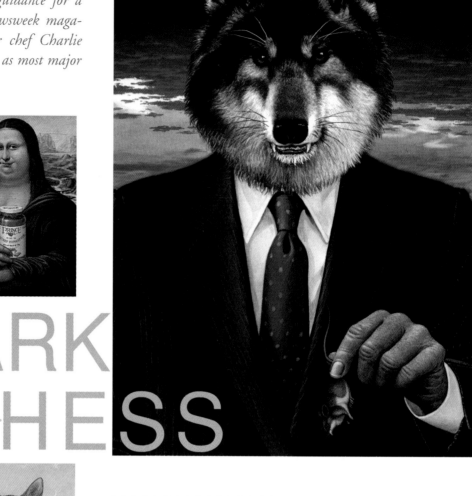

TIM O'BRIEN

LOTT REPRESENTATIVES · 212-954-7088

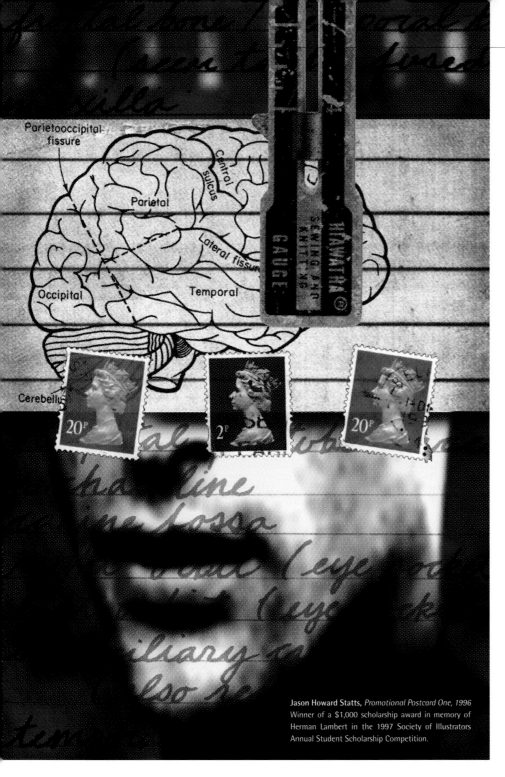

ARCHITECTURAL HISTORY

ARCHITECTURE

ART HISTORY

COMPUTER ART

FASHION

FIBERS

FURNITURE DESIGN

GRAPHIC DESIGN

HISTORIC PRESERVATION

ILLUSTRATION

INDUSTRIAL DESIGN

INTERIOR DESIGN

METALS AND JEWELRY

PAINTING

PHOTOGRAPHY

SEQUENTIAL ART

VIDEO

BACHELOR *of* FINE ARTS

MASTER *of* FINE ARTS

MASTER *of* ARTS

BACHELOR *of* ARCHITECTURE

MASTER *of* ARCHITECTURE

Jason Howard Statts, *Promotional Postcard One, 1996*
Winner of a $1,000 scholarship award in memory of
Herman Lambert in the 1997 Society of Illustrators
Annual Student Scholarship Competition.

ABOUT THE COLLEGE

The Savannah College of Art and Design exists for the purpose of preparing talented students for careers in the visual arts, design, building arts, and the history of art and architecture. The college is a private, non-profit, tax-exempt institution accredited by the Commission on Colleges of the Southern Association of Colleges and Schools (1866 Southern Lane, Decatur, Georgia 30033-4097; telephone number 404-679-4501) to award bachelor's and master's degrees. The college offers bachelor of fine arts, master of arts and master of fine arts degrees in architectural history, art history, computer art, fibers, fashion, furniture design, graphic design, historic preservation, illustration, industrial design, interior design, metals and jewelry,

painting, photography, sequential art and video. The college also offers the bachelor of architecture degree and the master of architecture degree. The five-year bachelor of architecture degree is accredited by the National Architectural Accrediting Board. Minors are offered in architectural history, art history, electronic design, media and performing arts, printmaking and sound design.

For more information about the college, programs of study, or cultural events the college sponsors, call 1-800-869-7223 or visit the college on the World Wide Web at http://www.scad.edu. E-mail may be sent to info@scad.edu.

Savannah College *of* Art *and* Design

POST OFFICE BOX 3146 · SAVANNAH, GEORGIA · 31402-3146 USA

1 - 8 0 0 - 8 6 9 - 7 2 2 3 or 9 1 2 - 2 3 8 - 2 4 8 3 · W W W . S C A D . E D U · I N F O @ S C A D . E D U

Kirchoff/

Illustration © 1997 Daniel Moreton
FROM LA CUCARACHA MARTINA: A CARIBBEAN FOLKTALE
RETOLD AND ILLUSTRATED BY Daniel Moreton
PUBLISHED BY Turtle Books

Artists Representatives

Wohlberg

866 United Nations Plaza, New York, NY 10017   212-644-2020

the
DIRECTORY OF ILLUSTRATION
GENERATES BUSINESS

The Graphic Artists Guild's *Directory of Illustration* is not only an award-winning source book, but has also established a solid reputation for generating business for our advertisers.

Renewal advertising for the current edition of the *Directory of Illustration* has again set a record. Repeat advertiser business is the most important indicator that the *Directory of Illustration* is meeting our advertisers' needs for generating high paying jobs in a very competitive market.

The *Directory of Illustration* places your work among the *best* in the business. Many of the most respected artists and largest artist representation firms are participating in this year's edition.

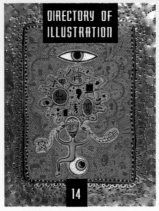

If your company is not receiving the *Directory of Illustration* and spends at least $50,000 per year on commercial illustration talent, you may qualify for a complimentary copy of this valuable source book. Please inquire for further information.

As an illustrator, advertising in the *Directory of Illustration* places your work among the *best* in the business. For more information on how the *Directory of Illustration* can help your business grow, please call for our 16-page brochure.

SAINT BERNARD

FIND WHO FITS

Seven Joanies

Picasso

Merchant Adventurer

Hanson

Garrett

Sorren

Swift

apJones

Molloy

JOanie Bernstein - artist representative - 612.374.3169

Tasty.

Coming to art directors' desks February 1, 1998

HOWARD CARTER AND THE MUMMY'S MAKE-UP CASE

Obsessed even more with grooming than they were with death, the
ancient Egyptians loaded their tombs with perfumes, hair oils and other beauty aids
that they'd need to spruce up in the afterlife. Pictured here, the famed archaeologist
Howard Carter struggles to recover the worlds first Samsonite make-up case.

Dennis Dittrich 212-343-0096

395 Broadway   Suite 10A   New York N.Y. 10013

Jean Craighead George

Arctic Son

PAINTINGS BY WENDELL MINOR

Hyperion Books for Children

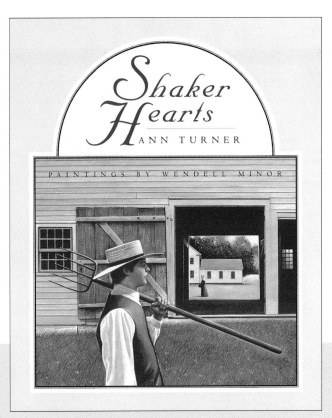

Shaker Hearts

ANN TURNER

PAINTINGS BY WENDELL MINOR

HarperCollins Publishers

"Surveying Minor's work, it's easy to see why writers are in awe of him: He's an artist in total command of his craft."—PEOPLE MAGAZINE

Visit Wendell Minor at http://www.minorart.com

Clarion Books

Browndeer Press / Harcourt Brace

RED FOX RUNNING
by Eve Bunting

Paintings by Wendell Minor

Grassroots

POEMS BY CARL SANDBURG

PAINTINGS BY WENDELL MINOR

SOCIETY
ACTIVITIES

• •

STEVAN DOHANOS AWARD Jerry Pinkney

OUR OWN SHOW
1997

THE SOCIETY OF ILLUSTRATORS
MEMBERS EIGHTH ANNUAL
OPEN EXHIBITION

"Our Own Show" is pleased to inaugurate the Stevan Dohanos Award
as the Best in Show in this open, unjuried exhibition.

"Our Own Show" was created to extend this annual opportunity for all professionally active members of the Society to exhibit a work in the Museum galleries. Each year nearly 200 artists participate.

AWARD OF MERIT David Bowers

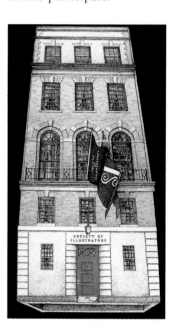

"Our Own Show" is the major funding source for the Ten Year Rebuilding plan which is modernizing the Society's 1875 Carriage House headquarters for the 21st Century.

AWARD OF MERIT Donato Giancola

ILLUSTRATORS 40

CALL FOR ENTRIES

THE 40TH ANNUAL EXHIBITION
INTERNATIONAL CATEGORY
DEADLINE: FEBRUARY 13, 1998

ILLUSTRATION BY LEO & DIANE DILLON   DESIGN BY WENDELL MINOR

SOCIETY OF ILLUSTRATORS · 128 EAST 63RD STREET · NEW YORK, NY 10021 · USA
FAX 011-212-838-2561 · WWW.SOCIETYILLUSTRATORS.ORG

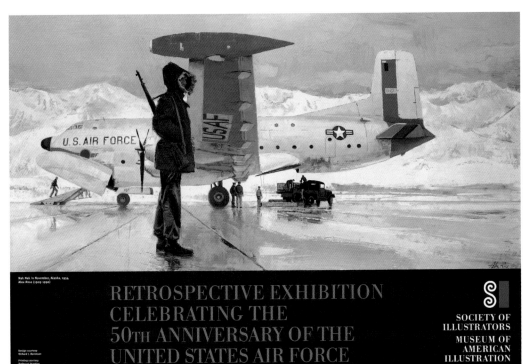

Nak Nek In November, Alaska, 1954
Alex Ross (1909-1990)

RETROSPECTIVE EXHIBITION
CELEBRATING THE
50TH ANNIVERSARY OF THE
UNITED STATES AIR FORCE
SEPTEMBER 3 THROUGH SEPTEMBER 27, 1997

Design courtesy
Richard L. Berntson
Printing courtesy
Preferred Printing
So. Norwalk, CT
Artwork courtesy
United States Air Force Art Collection
© Society of Illustrators 1997

SOCIETY OF
ILLUSTRATORS
MUSEUM OF
AMERICAN
ILLUSTRATION
128 EAST 63RD STREET
NEW YORK, NY 10021

Nak Nek in November, Alaska, 1954, Alex Ross (1909-1990). Artwork courtesy United States Air Force Art Collection. © Society of Illustrators 1997

1997 marked the 50th anniversary of the U. S. Air Force as a separate military service. To honor this occasion, a special retrospective exhibition of paintings and drawings produced for the Air Force from 1954 to the present time was held from September 3rd through the 29th at the Society of Illustrators. This vast exhibit was made up of work produced by Society members traveling with the Air Force across the nation and around the globe.

In exchange for transportation and hospitality, artists donated their work to the Air Force at formal

"The Hunter" - © Doug Smith

presentation dinners held in Washington, DC in October. Artists retain the copyrights in the work they contribute. The artwork is used for government purposes only.

Thus far the Air Force Art Collection has over 7000 works of art that will be a valuable documentation of the history of the U. S. Air Force.

Gil Cohen
Government Services Chair

"F-15, Keflavik, Iceland" - © Peter Fiore

SOCIETY OF ILLUSTRATORS
GOVERNMENT SERVICES COMMITTEE

128 East 63rd Street • New York, NY 10021-7303 • phone (212) 838-2560 • fax (212) 838-2561
EMail: society@societyillustrators.org

if you join now, you can come in and yell at the chef

Harry Beckhoff, *Collier's Magazine*. circa 1940, Courtesy of Illustration House

call it a membership perk

Great lunches and a chance to scream at the cook are just two
small facets of your membership in the Society of Illustrators.
If you are reading this annual, chances are you are part of
the graphic arts community, and are eligible for membership
in one of the following categories: Artist; Associate; Corporate;
Educator; Student or Friend of the Museum.

For details, call or write the Society and ask for a membership packet.

Oh, another perk is the friends you'll make.
So you won't have to yell at the chef alone.

SOCIETY OF ILLUSTRATORS

128 East 63rd Street • New York, NY 10021-7303 • (212) 838-2560 • fax (212) 838-2561
EMail: society@societyillustrators.org

SOCIETY OF ILLUSTRATORS MUSEUM SHOP

The Society of Illustrators Museum of American Illustration maintains a shop featuring many quality products. Four-color, large format books document contemporary illustration and the great artists of the past. Museum quality prints and posters capture classic images. T-shirts, sweatshirts, hats, mugs and tote bags make practical and fun gifts.

The Museum Shop is an extension of the Society's role as the center for illustration in America today. For further information or quantity discounts, contact the Society at
TEL: (212) 838-2560 / FAX: (212) 838-2561
EMail: society@societyillustrators.org

ILLUSTRATORS ANNUAL BOOKS

These catalogs are based on our annual juried exhibitions, divided into four major categories in American Illustration: Editorial, Book, Advertising, and Institutional. Some are available in a limited supply only.

In addition, a limited number of out-of-print collector's editions of the Illustrators Annuals that are not listed below (1959 to Illustrators 30) are available as is.

Also available for collectors are back issues of The Art Directors Club annuals and GRAPHIS Annuals.

Contact the Society for details...

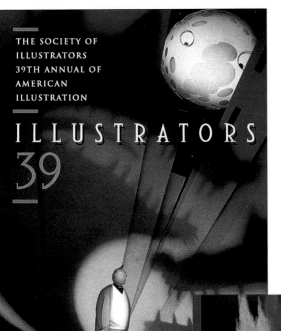

NEW!

ILLUSTRATORS 39
320 pp.
Cover by Bill Mayer
Contains 489 works of art.
Included are Hall of Fame biographies
and the Hamilton King interview.
Our most recent annual, the most
contemporary illustration.
$57.50

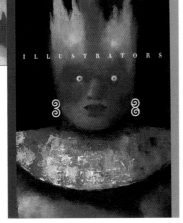

ILLUSTRATORS 38
$40.00

ILLUSTRATORS 37
$40.00

ILLUSTRATORS 36
$35.00

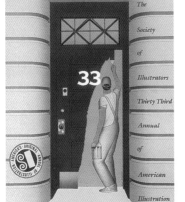

ILLUSTRATORS 33
$25.00
limited number remaining

ILLUSTRATORS 32
$20.00
limited number remaining

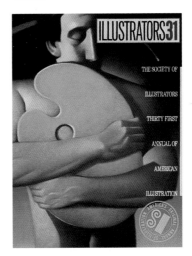

ILLUSTRATORS 31
$20.00
limited number remaining

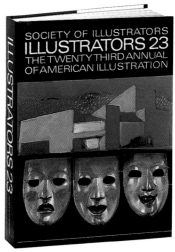

ILLUSTRATORS 23
$20.00
limited number remaining

Raúl Colón

**ARTISTS FEATURED
IN THE SERIES:**

EDITORIAL

Marshall Arisman

Guy Billout

Alan E. Cober

Elaine Duillo

Joan Hall

Wilson McLean

Barbara Nessim

Tim O'Brien

Mel Odom

ADVERTISING

N. Ascencios

Mark Borow

Robert M. Cunningham

Teresa Fasolino

Mark Hess

Hiro Kimura

Rafal Olbinski

Fred Otnes

Chris Spollen

CHILDREN'S BOOKS

Steve Byram

Raúl Colón

Laura Cornell

Steve Kroninger

Emily McCully

James McMullan

Jerry Pinkney

Charles Santore

Dan Yaccarino

Jerry Pinkney

Guy Billout

Fred Otnes

PRO-ILLUSTRATION
by Jill Bossert
A New How-to Series

VOLUME ONE

EDITORIAL ILLUSTRATION $24.00

The Society of Illustrators has simulated an editorial assignment for a Sunday magazine supplement surveying the topic of "Love." Topics assigned to the illustrators include: Erotic Love, First Love, Weddings, Sensual Love, Computer Love, Adultery and Divorce. The stages of execution. from initial sketch to finish, are shown in a series of photographs and accompanying text. It's a unique, behind-the-scenes look at each illustrator's studio and the secrets of their individual styles. Professional techniques demonstrated include oil, acrylic, collage, computer, etching, trompe l'oeil, dyes and airbrush.

Joan Hall

Chris Spollen

VOLUME TWO

ADVERTISING ILLUSTRATION $24.00

This is an advertising campaign for a fictitious manufacturer of timepieces. The overall concept is "Time" and nine of the very best illustrators put their talents to solving the problem. The stages of execution, from initial phone call to finish, are described in photographs and text. You'll understand the demonstration of the techniques used to create a final piece of art. Professional techniques demonstrated include oil, acrylic, mixed media collage, computer, three-dimension and airbrush.

VOLUME THREE

CHILDREN'S BOOKS $24.00

In photographs and text, each of the nine artists describe the stages of execution from initial idea--if they are the author, too--or manuscript proposed by an editor, to the completion of a piece of art. They discuss the special challenges of creating children's books, among them: consistency of character and tone, attention to pace and visual flow, and the task of serving narrative as well as aesthetics.

Charles Santore

Maxfield Parrish • J. C. Leyendecker • Norman Rockwell • N. C. Wyeth • James Montgomery Flagg • Dean Cornwell
Harold Von Schmidt • Al Parker • Robert Fawcett • Stevan Dohanos • Tom Lovell • Charles Dana Gibson
Bernie Fuchs • Winslow Homer • Robert Peak • Coby Whitmore • Frederic Remington • Howard Chandler Christy
John Clymer • Mark English • Charles Marion Russell • Rockwell Kent • Al Hirschfeld • Haddon Sundblom
Maurice Sendak • René Bouché • Robert T. McCall • John Held, Jr. • Burt Silverman • Jessie Willcox Smith • Joe Bowler
Dorothy Hood • Robert McGinnis • Thomas Nast • Coles Phillips • Ben Shahn • McClelland Barclay
and many, many more

FAMOUS AMERICAN ILLUSTRATORS

NEW!

by Arpi Ermoyan

THE HALL OF FAME

Every year since the inception of the Hall of Fame in 1958, the Society of Illustrators bestows its highest honor upon those artists recognized for their distinguished achievement in the art of illustration. The 87 recipients of the Hall of Fame Award represented in this book are the foremost illustrators of the last two centuries.

FAMOUS AMERICAN ILLUSTRATORS, a full-color, 224 page volume, is a veritable "Who's Who" of American illustration. The artists are presented in the order in which they were elected to the Hall of Fame. Included are short biographical sketches and major examples of each artist's work. Their range of styles is all-encompassing, their viewpoints varied, their palettes imaginative. The changing patterns of life in America are vividly recorded as seen through the eyes of these men and women—the greatest illustrators of the 19th and 20th Centuries. **11 1-2 x 12 inches. $49.95**

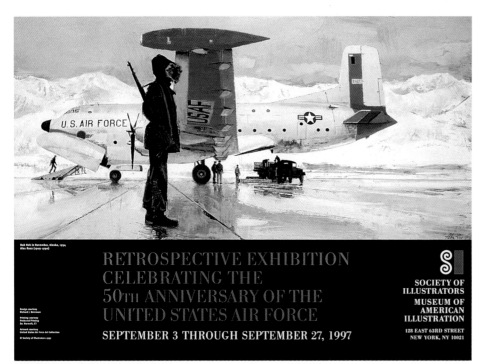

US AIR FORCE RETROSPECTIVE - Alex Ross - 25" x 19" $10.00

EUGENE HOFFMAN 3-D Art - 26" x 31" $10.00

THE DIGITAL SHOW - Steve Lyons
15" x 27" $10.00

EDWIN AUSTIN ABBEY   25" x 22" $10.00

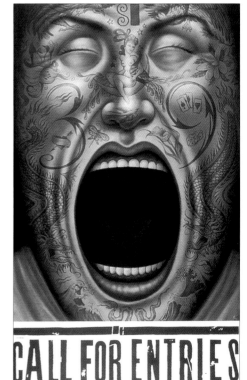

39TH ANNUAL - A. Kunz - 22" x 38" $10.00

POSTERS

The Society has created some of the most exciting and enjoyable posters around to announce their exhibitions. Subjects are both contemporary and historic. All are full color and are printed on premium stock.

The set of 7 posters: $35.00

DONALD MOSS
22" x28"
$10.00

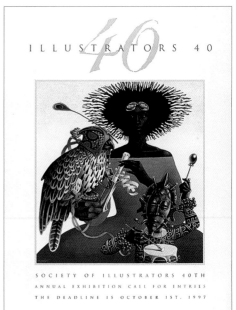

40TH ANNUAL
Leo & Diane Dillon
18" x 24" $10.00

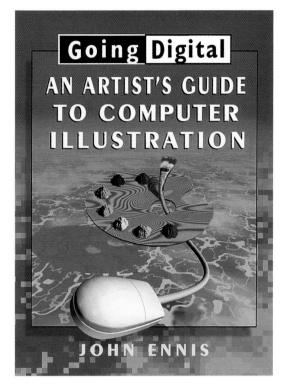

THE BUSINESS OF ILLUSTRATION
Steve Heller's effective text on the nuts and bolts and whys of illustration. Commentary by leading pros and agents as well as hints on pricing and self-promotion. Great for students and young professionals. Recommended highly.
144 pages, softbound, color **$27.50**

GOING DIGITAL
AN ARTIST'S GUIDE TO COMPUTER ILLUSTRATION
At last, an easy-to-read guide to illustrating on your computer. Author and illustrator, John Ennis, offers an under- the-hood look at how it's done and how to start up your digital studio.
144 pages, softbound, color. **$29.95**

HEALTH HAZARDS MANUAL
A comprehensive review of materials and supplies, from fixatives to pigments, airbrushes to solvents.
132 pages, softbound. **$9.95**

THE BUSINESS LIBRARY

Each of these volumes is a valuable asset to the professional artist whether established or just starting out. Together they form a solid base for your business.

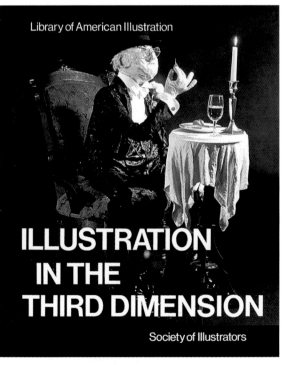

ILLUSTRATION IN THE THIRD DIMENSION
27 artists explain just how dimensional art works. Media include woods, metals, fabrics, resins and junk. This 1978 classic is still an effective look at this genre.
112 pages, hardbound, limited color. **$12.00**

THE LEGAL GUIDE FOR THE VISUAL ARTIST
1997 EDITION.
Tad Crawford's text explains basic copyrights, moral rights, the sale of rights, taxation, business accounting and the legal support groups available to artists.
256 pages, softbound. **$18.95**

GRAPHIC ARTISTS GUILD HANDBOOK PRICING AND ETHICAL GUIDELINES - VOL. 10
Includes an outline of ethical standards and business practices, as well as price ranges for hundreds of uses and sample contracts.
312 page, softbound. **$24.95**

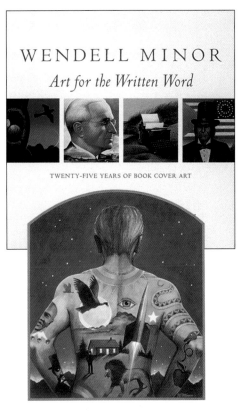

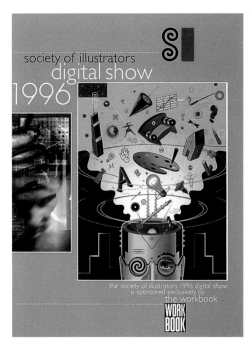

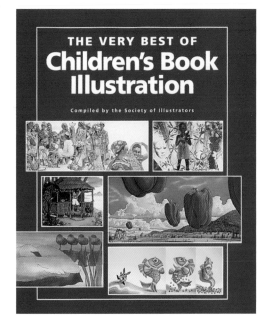

**WENDELL MINOR
ART FOR THE WRITTEN WORD**
A retrospective of this award-winning
artist's book cover art. Includes an
introduction by David McCullough
and commentary by the authors.
154 pages, color, softbound.
$30.00

SI DIGITAL SHOW
The Society's recent exhibition of the computer
as media. 44 current artists show a wide range
of stylistic approaches using different software
and hardware. Includes Show Chairs and
Jurors comments.
36 pages, color, softbound. **$10.00**

A retrospective of Illustrated children's books from
1992. This volume contains valuable "how-to"
comments from the artists as well as a publishers
directory. A compilation of the exhibition, "The Original
Art 1992 - Celebrating the Fine Art of Children's Book
Illustration."
136 pages, color, hardbound. **$29.95**

BOOKS & CATALOGS

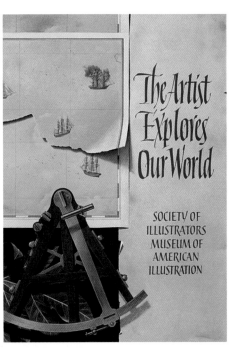

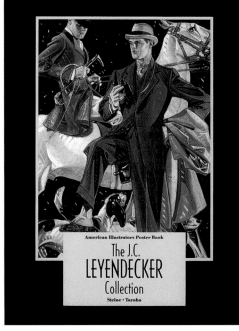

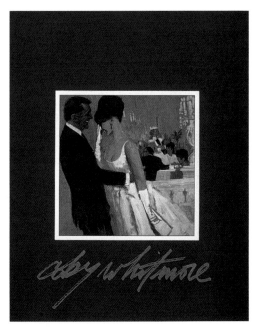

THE ARTIST EXPLORES OUR WORLD
The catalog of National Geographic's
Centennial Exhibition. Includes biographical
sketches of 44 artists and color samples
of most.
16 pages, color, softbound. **$10.00**

THE J. C. LEYENDECKER COLLECTION
Collector's Press poster edition offering 18 plates
all from the original art with accompanying text by
Fred Taraba. An outstanding addition for the
discerning collector.
22 pages, color. 10" x 14". **$24.95**

COBY WHITMORE
The good life of the 1950s and 1960s as illustrated in
the Ladies Home Journal, McCall's and Redbook.
12 pages, color, softbound. **$16.00**

APPAREL

SI CAPS
Blue or Red with SI logo and name
embroidered in white.
Adjustable,
one size fits all
$15.

White shirt with the Society logo.
L, XL, XXL **$15.**

39TH ANNUAL EXHIBITION "CALL" T-SHIRT
Image of the tattooed face by Anita Kunz.
100% cotton. Heavyweight pocket T.
L, XL, XXL **$15.**

**38TH ANNUAL EXHIBITION
"CALL" T-SHIRT**
Image of a frog on a palette by Jack Unruh.
Frog on front pocket.
100% cotton. Heavyweight pocket T.
L, XL, XXL **$15.**

SWEATSHIRTS
Blue with white lettering of multiple
logos or grey with large red SI.
L, XL, XXL **$20.**

40TH ANNUAL EXHIBITION "CALL" T-SHIRT
Image of "The Messenger" by Leo and Diane Dillon.
100% cotton. Heavyweight pocket T.
L, XL, XXL **$15.**

GIFT ITEMS

SI LAPEL PINS
Actual Size
$6.00

The Society's famous Red and Black logo, designed by Bradbury Thompson, is featured on many items.

SI TOTE BAGS
Heavyweight, white canvas bags are 14" high with the two-color logo **$15.00**

SI PATCH
White with blue lettering and piping - 4" wide
$4.00

SI CERAMIC COFFEE MUGS
Heavyweight 14 oz. mugs feature the Society's logo or original illustrations from the Permanent Collection.
1. John Held, Jr.'s "Flapper";
2. Norman Rockwell's "Dover Coach";
3. J. C. Leyendecker's "Easter";
4. Charles Dana Gibson's "Gibson Girl"
5. SI Logo
$6.00 each

SI NOTE CARDS
Norman Rockwell greeting cards, 3-7/8" x 8-5/8", inside blank, great for all occasions. Includes 100% rag envelopes

10 CARDS - $10.00
20 CARDS - $18.00
50 CARDS - $35.00
100 CARDS - $60.00

ORDER FORM

Mail: The Museum Shop, Society of Illustrators, 128 East 63rd Street, New York, NY 10021-7303
Phone: 1-800-SI-MUSEUM (1-800-746-8738) Fax: 1-212-838-2561 EMail: society@societyillustrators.org

39

NAME _____

COMPANY _____

STREET _____
(No P.O. Box numbers please)

CITY _____

STATE _____ ZIP _____

PHONE ( ) _____

Enclosed is my check for $ _____
Make checks payable to SOCIETY OF ILLUSTRATORS

Please charge my credit card:

☐ American Express   ☐ Master Card   ☐ Visa

CARD NUMBER _____

SIGNATURE _____ EXPIRATION DATE _____
*please note if name appearing on the card is different than the mailing name.

Ship via FEDEX Economy and charge my account _____

QTY	DESCRIPTION	SIZE	COLOR	PRICE	TOTAL
# of items ordered			Total price of item(s) ordered		
			TAX (NYS Residents add 8 1/4%)		
			UPS Shipping per order		6.00
			or		
			Foreign Shipping per order		15.00
			or		
					FX
			TOTAL DUE		

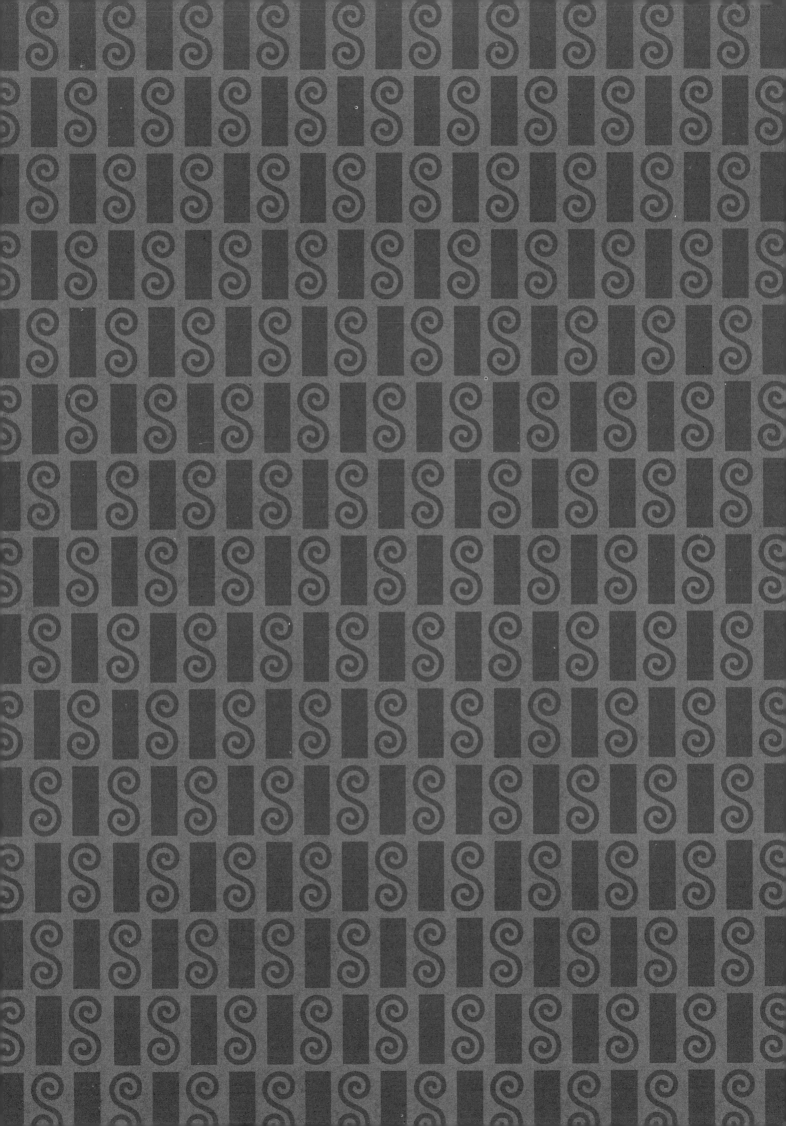